D0014612

THE
MONEY
PLAYBOOK

amplify

www.amplifypublishing.com

The Money Playbook: The Professional Athlete's Guide to Building Lifelong Wealth

©2022 Mark M. Tepper, CFP®. All Rights Reserved. No part of this publication may be reproduced, stored in a retrieval system or transmitted in any form by any means electronic, mechanical, or photocopying, recording or otherwise without the permission of the author.

Although the author and publisher have made every effort to ensure that the information in this book was correct at press time, the author and publisher do not assume and hereby disclaim any liability to any party for any loss, damage, or disruption caused by errors or omissions, whether such errors or omissions result from negligence, accident, or any other cause.

For more information, please contact:
Amplify, an imprint of Amplify Publishing Group
620 Herndon Parkway #320
Herndon, VA 20170
info@amplifypublishing.com

Library of Congress Control Number: 2021913793

CPSIA Code: PRV0422A
ISBN-13: 978-1-64543-932-5

Printed in the United States

To my clients, the Strategic Wealth Partners team, and most of all my family—my heartfelt thanks.

THE MONEY PLAYBOOK

THE PROFESSIONAL ATHLETE'S GUIDE TO BUILDING LIFELONG WEALTH

MARK M. TEPPER, CFP®

amplify

CONTENTS

MONEY CHANGES EVERYTHING

According to Bleacher Report, only one in two hundred high school baseball players will get drafted by a Major League team. That's one-half of one percent. Then, only 10 to 15 percent of those who were drafted will actually make it to the big leagues. The odds of a high school football player being drafted by an NFL team are even longer, about one in four thousand. According to the 2018–2019 High School Athletics Participation Survey, more than one million kids played high school football in those years, but just 254 donned a logo cap on draft day.

That's nothing compared to the odds of a young player making it from high school basketball to the NBA. More than 540,000 kids suited up in high school gyms in 2018–2019, but only sixty were drafted. That means the odds of going from high school to play alongside James Harden and LeBron James are around one in *nine thousand*. You can fiddle with the numbers a little when you factor in international drafts and the like, but the basic math doesn't change: the *vast* majority of teens who dream about being professional athletes will never get there.

So, congratulations. You're one of the elite few who've made it.

You're a professional athlete. It doesn't matter if you're playing in the bright spotlight of MLB, the NBA, NFL, or NHL, suiting up in Major League Soccer or the WNBA, competing on the PGA Tour, or traveling for ATP tennis. You could be developing your craft in minor league baseball or some lesser-known pro league or going it alone in a sport like surfing, triathlon, or cycling. There are hundreds of ways to be a pro athlete, but you've done it. You've taken talent and determination, added God knows how many hours of grueling work, and built a career.

So, what now? Well, the clock is ticking. One of the factors that makes pro athletes different from professionals in any other field is that your careers are a lot shorter, so your earning window is a lot shorter too. Musicians, writers, and other artists can and do work into their eighties and beyond. Even people working in fields that require physical labor, like firefighters and police officers, routinely work into their sixties. But if you're a pro athlete, you're extremely lucky if you're still earning a paycheck after the calendar flips to forty.

Heck, *thirty*.

So let's talk about the income you actually earn. If you're on a roster in the NBA, NFL, Major League Baseball, or the NHL, you're probably doing pretty well between salary, endorsements, and bonuses. But if you're in a sport that's further from the mainstream, it might be a little harder to make ends meet. Let's look at the numbers:

- **UFC.** The cream of the mixed martial arts crop, such as Stipe Miocic or Conor McGregor, make huge money in the sport from prize purses and endorsements. For example, as of 2019 Miocic's net worth was estimated at $29 million, while McGregor was worth an estimated $120 million. However, they're the outliers. According to TheStreet, the average UFC fighter earns about $138,000 a year—not bad, but not "set for life" territory either.

- **Running.** According to estimates published by LetsRun.com, pro track and field athlete salaries range from $32,000 to $237,000 per year. Pro men's marathoners go from a low of $10,000 to a high of around $141,667.

- **Cycling.** While there are some pro cyclists who make huge money because of big sponsor and endorsement deals, as well as purses for events like the Tour de France, according to ZipRecruiter the average pro cyclist in the US makes $56,652 a year.

- **Triathlon.** A 2010 survey by USA Triathlon found that the average professional triathlete earned about $128,000 a year.

- **Tennis.** Online magazine *The Conversation* found that pro tennis has one of the highest levels of income inequality of any sport. While a tiny sliver of top players can earn millions, and the top 125 pro tennis players earn an average of about $400,000 annually, around 80 percent of pros earn almost nothing.

- **Golf.** According to *Golf* magazine, the average PGA tour pro ranked among the top 125 players will take home about $2 million a year. A large chunk of that comes from deals for the logo on the hat he wears, the clubs he uses, the ball he uses, and the shoes he wears.

- **Soccer.** Career Trend said in 2013 that the average salary for players in Major League Soccer was $148,693.26.

- **Baseball.** Now we start getting into the high-rent district: MLB says that the average player salary in 2019 was $3,894,220.

- **Football.** The average salary for an NFL player is about $2.9 million, according to the *Los Angeles Times*, though they say that the monster salaries of the top-tier players skew that number disproportionately.

- **Hockey.** According to Statista, the average National Hockey League player laces up his skates to the tune of $2.71 million.

- **Basketball.** Pro hoops are at the top of the heap. CNBC says the average NBA player takes home a cool $7.7 million a year.

Now, set those numbers aside, because they aren't real. Wait, why not? Lots of reasons. First, *disparity*. There's a world of difference between Mike Trout and a first-year utility infielder for the Miami Marlins. Second, *expenses*. It costs money to be a pro athlete: commissions, personal trainers and coaches, equipment, travel, you name it. Third, *volatility*. In some sports like tennis, golf, and cycling, if you pull a hamstring and can't compete, you don't get paid. If you hit a cold streak, you don't get paid. But your bills keep coming.

Plus, quite simply, not every athlete makes big money. In fact, most don't. Mike Golic, who spent nine years in the NFL as a defensive lineman with the Houston Oilers, Philadelphia Eagles, and Miami Dolphins before joining ESPN, talked about his experience in our interview. "I got hurt my senior year at Notre Dame," he said. "It was trending that I might have been drafted in the first couple of rounds, and then I got hurt the first game of my senior year. I played sparingly my senior year, and I got shoulder surgery at the end of it. So I went to the combine, but I couldn't do anything. I ended up going in the tenth round. My base salary was $62,000, and I got a $17,500 signing bonus. So obviously nowhere near what the guys get today. Even back then, it wasn't a lot of money." For perspective, if you assume 3 percent inflation, a $62,000 salary back then is equivalent to about $175,000 today. That's far below even today's NFL minimum salary of $600,000. In those days, making the League didn't mean you were set for life, not by a long shot.

Finally, there's the big one: *your expiration date*. Pro sports careers rarely last long and can end in a second with a torn ACL or a fastball to the head. The average NFL career is about three years; the average NBA career, about four-and-a-half years. For every guy who's signing a

$100 million contract that sets him and his family up for life, there are a hundred players who work their asses off, play for a few years, and then move on to the next stage of their lives. But imagine being thirty-three years old, with your whole life ahead of you and the only job you've ever had gone, with maybe $10,000 in the bank and no idea what to do next.

That happened to NFL running back Merril Hoge. After seven solid seasons with the Pittsburgh Steelers, he signed with the Chicago Bears in 1994 but suffered successive concussions that led to a brief cardiac arrest and other severe symptoms that forced him out of the game at twenty-nine. Now what? Merril explained in our interview:

> You can't predict when injury could happen. Anything could end your career at any time, so you can't worry about that. I was lucky that I had Chuck Noll, an icon, a once-in-a-lifetime man to share wisdom with me for five years. Thankfully I was smart enough, even at twenty-one, to realize I didn't know everything and that I ought to pay attention.
>
> Walter Payton and I had a great discussion on this one time, and I learned a lot of things from Walter on how he trained. In sports the only things you can control are being in phenomenal shape, being awesome at your craft, and playing as hard as you can. You can't control injuries. My goal was to play ten years, and technically that would have happened 'cause I had just signed a three-year deal, and that would have taken me to ten years. I had that same type of philosophy—phenomenal shape, play as hard as you can, and be good at your craft. But you also have to be smart. If something happens that's out of your control, you can still prepare for your life's work. You can use the stage that you have. Chuck Noll talked a lot about this.
>
> He always said, "Use the stage, don't abuse it," and what he meant by that was that in the off-season, if you can get your schooling done, get it done. If you're interested in some other

craft or passion, explore it. In the NFL they create all kinds of platforms for you. Now you can start branding yourself or learning about different things. Before I had any resources, that's what I did. My dad went from a milkman to a New York Life insurance agent, and I said, "Let's look into that." It took me one visit. When the guy dropped off about ten books for me to read, I said, "Well, this ain't me," and I went into broadcasting.

WRITING A REALITY CHECK

It's in your power to keep your financial wake-up call from being ugly, even if your career does end suddenly. Are you blessed with gifts? *Yes*. Have you sacrificed and sweated to get to the pros? *Yes*. Does that mean you don't ever have to worry about money again? *No.* Because even the stars who sign the $100 million contracts can go broke if they make bad financial decisions and trust the wrong people.

Take Vin Baker. Drafted eighth by the Milwaukee Bucks of the NBA and a four-time All-Star, he earned nearly $100 million in his career. But he also developed a substance abuse problem and spent recklessly, and by 2006, he was out of the league and broke. Baker ended up working at Starbucks for $900 a week before finally turning his life around and making it back to the NBA as a coach.

Stories like this are distressingly common. Hall of Fame defensive tackle Warren Sapp admits to blowing $82 million, while former NBA star Antoine Walker reportedly torched $108 million. An infamous *Sports Illustrated* story claimed that 78 percent of retired NFL players and 60 percent of retired NBA players are either broke or having serious financial problems within five years of hanging 'em up. There are some doubts about how accurate those numbers are, but a great many pro athletes reach the earning cliff at the end of their careers unprepared to do anything but jump and hope for a soft landing. And hope is not a strategy.

I don't want any of that to happen to you. That's why I've written this book.

Here's the first thing you need to understand. The financial nemesis of the professional athlete isn't overspending or scandal or injury or not making enough money. It's *the belief that you're invincible*. It's assuming that because you're earning a nice living in your sport, things will either "work out" or someone will come along to take care of your money so you don't have to. It's believing that you don't have to learn the basics of investing, debt, and taxes. It's the refusal to accept certain realities:

- After taxes, commissions, and expenses, you're lucky if fifty cents of every dollar you earn makes it into your checking account.

- Being an athlete is a full-time job, so even if you're interested in learning about finance and investing, you don't have time to manage the details of your financial life. That means you have to trust someone. If it's the wrong someone, you're in trouble.

- Being a pro athlete and having money makes you a target for scammers, online trolls, the tabloids, and unethical money managers.

- When you quit playing, the money doesn't slow gradually. It *stops*. It falls off a cliff. Most of your endorsements and sponsorships will end. Even if you have a post-career plan, you could easily see an 80 or 90 percent drop in your income virtually overnight.

- Sports change. Remember when running backs were a big deal in the NFL? Now it's a passing game, and quarterbacks like Patrick Mahomes get the big bucks. In the NBA, the low post game of Shaq used to dominate, but now it's all about the three-pointer. It's possible to wake up one day and find out you can't get a contract because you're irrelevant.

- Even if you defy the odds, get a nice contract, stay healthy, and play until you can retire on your own terms, what then? If you don't make plans, you're an ex-jock with no marketable skills.

YOU'RE NOT AN ATHLETE; YOU'RE AN ENTERPRISE

The career of a professional athlete represents a brief, blessed slice of time when you have incredible prestige, visibility, and earning power. The biggest mistake you can make is to act like that slice of time is endless. It's not. Getting a nice signing bonus or a big free agent or endorsement contract is not enough to guarantee a lifetime of financial security for you and your family. It's only the first step. You need to use your prestige and visibility to pursue financial opportunities that will go on long after you've retired. You need to use the money you do make wisely, so some of it will grow in the form of investments and businesses.

The second thing you need to understand is that it's possible to do that even if you don't ever make huge money as a pro. One example is former NBA player Junior Bridgeman, who had a solid career with the Milwaukee Bucks and Los Angeles Clippers from 1975 to 1987. According to Money Maven, the most Bridgeman ever made in a season was $350,000. But today, according to Celebritynetworth.com, he has a net worth of about $600 million.

How? He purchased three Wendy's franchises while he was still playing, and after retirement, he continued buying franchises and getting his business education. Today he owns about 240 Wendy's restaurants and about 120 Chili's locations and is a bottler for Coca-Cola. He's an athlete who made a relatively modest salary, made smart financial decisions, and built lasting wealth—the polar opposite of Vin Baker.

This is the starting point of changing your thinking about money forever:

You are not an athlete. You are a business, and you need to handle your finances like one.

You're a brand. Your name, image, and reputation equal power that you can turn into a lifetime of financial success and security for you and your family. However, you have to start thinking and acting like a marketable brand and a business *today*. If you want to build sustainable wealth, it's time to start running your career like an enterprise.

You, the athlete, are the product of this enterprise. You're the iPhone. Yes, it's a fantastic product, but if Apple wants to stay alive to sell billions of iPhones, it has to run efficiently. The people who run the company can't be wasteful. They need to manage their balance sheet appropriately so they don't run out of cash and can maximize the return on their investments in marketing, R&D, and design. They need to hire good employees who handle day-to-day operations, who make sure taxes and bills are paid, spending is under control, and security is airtight. If you want to build something that will outlast your playing years, you must begin running your career and life the same way.

I'm going to show you how. I'm going to explain everything you need to do to build your Athlete Enterprise System (AES)™, the organizing structure that will get your life as organized and disciplined as a successful business and set you up for a financially independent retirement and a smooth transition to the next stage of your life.

FINANCIAL SECURITY IS ABOUT SMART DECISIONS

Creating a lifetime of financial security for yourself and your family is not about your income but about making a series of good choices. It's about educating yourself, whether by going to school in the off-season, getting your degree after your career ends, learning online, or attending one of the many financial and entrepreneurial boot camps put on by the pro leagues (more about those later).

It's about choosing the right people for your financial team. As you'll see, many athletes who lost everything did so because they trusted financial advisors or tax accountants who were either incompetent or corrupt. You'll need a team of skilled professionals who put your needs first. I'll show you how to choose them.

It's also about adopting everyday habits that are less about spending and more about saving: passing up flashy big-ticket purchases in favor of value, keeping your personal life in order, and above all, saving and investing as much as you can. That's more critical than you might realize, as I'll detail in the following example.

Suppose you're a superstar lucky enough to earn an average of $20 million a year over a ten-year career that ends when you're thirty-five. That's $200 million in gross income, big money. However, about 50 percent of that income goes to federal, state, and local taxes, and commissions to agents. You'll pay your overhead—publicists, personal trainers, personal chefs, and so on—out of the remaining 50 percent. So your net income is $100 million—still a lot, right? Yes, but many pro athletes become so overwhelmed by the numbers that they make a terrible mistake: *They assume that much money will last forever.* Trust me, it won't.

Let's assume you are disciplined enough to save half of that $10 million a year. That means you're spending $5 million a year on mortgages, cars, travel, entertainment, food, you name it. That's an awful lot of disposable income going out the door—too much, in my opinion, but for the sake of the example, let's roll with it. The other $5 million you invest in a portfolio of stocks, bonds, venture capital funds, and the like.

Look, I've owned Ferraris, Porsches, G-Wagons, Escalades, and the like, several at a time. I'll tell you, the novelty wears off fast. Then you're stuck with a bunch of depreciating assets that you don't drive. Fortunately, I was able to pull my head out of my ass and divest myself of most of them.

Rule of thumb: Your car payments shouldn't exceed 3 percent of your after-tax annual income, and 5 percent is the absolute ceiling. So if you're taking home $1 million after taxes, the max you should drop on car payments is $30,000 annually. Also, I don't recommend buying depreciating assets. Instead, lease your vehicles, unless you have your eye on one particular car that you plan on keeping for a very long time. To break it down:

- An $85,000 Escalade can be leased for payments of around $20,000 annually.
- A $150,000 G-Wagon can be leased for payments of $35,000 annually.
- A middle-of-the-road Porsche would lease out at around $25,000 per year.
- A Lamborghini Aventador is off-limits, buddy.

If you invested that $5 million each year and earned an annualized return of 7 percent, in ten years you would have turned $50 million into nearly $79 million. Not bad. That's your nest egg. But remember, you're thirty-five, you no longer have a contract with a professional sports team, and you have to turn that nest egg into a paycheck that will last your whole life. Most financial advisors suggest that you withdraw no more than 3 percent of your retirement assets per year if you want that money to last for the rest of your life, so that's what you take out each year to live on.

That's about $2.37 million. Okay, you can live nicely on that—but wait. You have to pay tax on your gains. You're in the top marginal tax bracket, and let's suppose you live in Denver, Colorado, which means you pay state income tax as well as federal income tax. If we assume you're filing as a married couple (and we ignore deductions and assume that all your gains are taxed as income rather than capital gains because that overcomplicates things), you would pay around $920,000 in federal and state taxes for the 2021 tax year. That drops you down to a net income of around $1.4 million.

True, nobody's going to throw you a pity party, but think about this. You did an awesome job of saving and investing, and your income *still* dropped from $5 million a year to $1.4 million a year after retirement—a 72 percent decline. Damn. And by pro athlete standards, that would be deemed a big success. Compare that with a retired executive, who might seek to replace 100 percent of his annual income in retirement and because he earned maybe $250,000 in a good year, is able to do that with relative ease. He doesn't experience a lifestyle drop-off, but you do.

That steep decline takes many pros by surprise. They don't think about what it means to be in their thirties with huge lifestyle expenses and no more income. It's a shock. But what if you weren't disciplined? What if you spent like a drunken sailor on multiple houses, Lambos, and all the other trappings and only saved $1 million per year? Over ten years at a 7 percent annualized rate of return, that $10 million would grow to about $14 million. Take out 3 percent, and that's about $420,000 a year. If you pay those same federal and Colorado state taxes, you're going from living like a high roller to living on about $314,000 per year. While that's a great living for most Americans, it could be a shock to a superstar athlete, especially if you've become accustomed to an expensive lifestyle. In other words, so much for your butler, your chef, your chauffeur, your security team, and your landscaper.

Now, what if you don't get ten years of maximum earnings? What if you only play five years and then your career is over?

The point is, whatever lifestyle you enjoy while you're playing, it's almost certain to decline after you stop playing, no matter how well you save your money. That's what happens to 90 percent of professional athletes. What about the other 10 percent?

They're the smart ones. They leverage their income, prestige, and contacts to plan for their post-playing future. They invest in the market and in private companies, buy franchises and real estate, build their brands as speakers, authors, and media figures, and even keep some of their endorsement and sponsorship deals after they retire—like Brett Favre did for Wrangler Jeans or Copper Fit compression sleeves. (Favre lost a lot of his sponsorship deals in 2011 when a texting scandal went public, but fortunately for him, he's kept some of his endorsements.)

If you want to experience little or no drop-off in your standard of living after your career is over—or even do like Junior Bridgeman did and make a lot more than you ever did during your playing days—the time to make good decisions, get educated, and put your team and plan in place is *now*, while you're still playing. The sooner, the better. If you wait until you hang up your cleats or skates for the last time, it's too late.

THINGS WILL STILL HAVE TO CHANGE

However, even if you make the smart decisions I'm going to teach you about and become a business-savvy, money-savvy athlete, you're still going to have to make changes. Here's what you'll have to take a hard look at, and why:

- **Your spending habits.** You can't throw cash around, take care of all the tabs, and run up monster credit card bills. When you're not paying attention, reckless spending adds up faster than you think.

- **Your private behavior.** If you're playing your social life cool, good for you. But if you're going to parties and strip clubs, acting up on social media, and getting in trouble, that can cost you in endorsements and more.

- **The people you hang with.** Some friends will want you to support them, others will want you to invest in their business ideas, and others will just get you into trouble by associating you with drugs, scandal, and crime. If you want to be a businessperson, a brand, or a media figure once you're done playing, it's time to drop the people who don't serve that goal.

- **How you think about yourself.** Being a pro athlete is special. Even if you're in a relatively small sport like surfing or triathlon, in that world and to those fans, you're a brand and a business. You have to think like one. That means reducing potential liability, building for the future, and running all your affairs like you're a company, with caution and restraint.

- **How you think about money.** When you get a big contract or prize purse, it's easy to forget that money is finite. It will run out. You can live like a Saudi prince for a while, but you're not one. If you want to set yourself and your family up for life, you need discipline and a plan for saving, investing, and having fun.

- **Your team.** I'm not talking about your sports team. I'm talking about the financial and business team you assemble, the professionals at the heart of your AES: your chief marketing officer (usually your agent), your chief financial officer (a credentialed financial advisor), and your chief operating officer (your business manager). They are your Board of Directors, and you're the CEO of You, Inc.

How do I know all this? Because for more than twenty years, I've been helping affluent individuals grow and protect their wealth through both bull markets and deep recessions. I'm a CERTIFIED FINANCIAL PLANNER™ professional, or CFP® professional, the gold standard in the world of financial advisors. I'm also an NFL Players Association Registered Player Financial Advisor. I went through an intense, ten-month-long background vetting process to gain approval. My portfolio of clients consists of pro athletes from every major sport, so I know the unique challenges you face. I've also been a regular on CNBC's *Fast Money*, *Closing Bell*, and *Power Lunch*, as well as on Fox Business. I've also published three other books: *Walk Away Wealthy—The Entrepreneur's Exit-Planning Playbook*, *Exceptional Wealth,* and an ebook called *Tilting the Odds*. The first two were Amazon bestsellers.

I'm here because there's too much misinformation around professional athletes and their financial planning, and I've seen too many athletes make irreversible financial mistakes because they got bad advice or not enough information. Too many financial professionals act as though all pro athletes are signing $100 million contracts and endorsement deals with Nike, when the reality is that most pros are more like working actors—making a solid living but not uber-rich superstars with mansions and yachts. And too many pro athletes misunderstand how long their money will last and don't know anything about subjects like taxes, running a small business, and hedge funds—subjects that will mean the difference between a post-career life of business, travel, enjoyment and comfortable affluence and . . . well, maybe working at Starbucks.

I've written *The Money Playbook* to fill in those gaps and to make sure as many pro athletes as possible are treated with the same attention and care as the superstars. If you're one of the elite few making $20 million a year or more, all I can say is, congratulations again! This book is a critical road map to turning that good fortune into a lifetime of financial security and freedom. But if you're one of the majority dedicated professional athletes making a good but not spectacular living doing what you love, this book is for you, too. Because if you want to enjoy life after sports as much as you enjoy playing, that starts now, with good information, making good decisions, and building a first-class personal Board of Directors to manage your financial life.

HOW THIS BOOK WORKS

The Money Playbook is about how to think about finances from the perspective of a professional athlete who is also a business. Chapter by chapter I'll walk you through how you should be thinking about every aspect of your financial life: the people you spend time with, the professionals you hire to manage your money, your private behavior, and of course, markets and investments. I'll go light on the financial jargon, but I'll tell you what you need to know, and I won't pull any punches. There's too much at stake, right?

I will also share with you some important tools for applying business thinking to your personal finances:

- **The Athlete Enterprise System.** An organizational plan for building your Board of Directors and running like a successful business all the way to and through retirement.

- **Financial Literacy for Athletes**. A series of more than forty bite-sized instructional videos I've recorded just for you at WealthLit101. com. Spend just ten minutes with each and you'll learn the essential basics of things like taxes, investing, the stock market, and a lot more.

- **The Athlete Income Planner**. This free software app lets you enter any income and spending amounts, automatically computes your taxes, and shows you how much you should be spending, saving, and investing to have the lifestyle you want.

Because there are many different kinds of athletes with many different kinds of careers, I've built the book around five basic "tracks," one of which I hope will capture where you are in your career:

1. **The Up-and-Comer.** This might be the rookie or the player who was just drafted. You're young and just starting out, so your annual earning power might be limited. We'll talk about ways to make the

most of what you earn and lay the groundwork for wealth no matter how long your career lasts.

2. **The Rising Star.** You're an experienced, still-young player with huge potential. You feel invincible and anticipate a long, lucrative career. We'll discuss factors that could make the difference between "comfortable for life" and "well, it's a number."

3. **The Solid Veteran.** You've been playing for years, and while you're probably not going to sign a nine-figure contract, you're making a healthy income. We'll look at how you can maximize it.

4. **The Sunsetting Veteran.** It's been a good run, but you're getting close to the end of your career. We'll dig into all the ways you can leverage career and business opportunities while you're still playing.

5. **The Soloist.** You're not on a team. You're Stipe Miocic or Jessica Evil Eye from the UFC. You're a pro tennis player, golfer, runner, cyclist, swimmer, or other solo athlete. Your income stream is different and so are your needs. We'll talk about the best ways to meet them.

My goal is to use my experience and all the tools I have described above to make you smarter about money and help you make all the right financial decisions during and after your pro career—especially in building your AES. That way, you can stop worrying about money, enjoy the ride, and thrive for the decades you'll have after your playing days are behind you. Let's get to it.

CHAPTER ONE

MASTERING THE FUNDAMENTALS

Kevin Garnett was one of the NBA's elite: an MVP, Defensive Player of the Year, league champ with the Boston Celtics, and one of the greatest power forwards of all time. No wonder his nickname was "The Big Ticket." But KG paid dearly for that big ticket when he trusted the wrong people to help him manage his finances. In 2018, Garnett sued his accountant, Michael Wertheim, and his accounting firm, Welenken CPAs, alleging that they had known Garnett's wealth manager, Charles Banks IV, had skimmed an incredible $77 million from Garnett's accounts and said nothing.

Why didn't the fifteen-time All-Star sue Banks? Because Banks was already doing four years in federal prison for defrauding another NBA superstar, Tim Duncan, out of $6 million back in 2012. But here's what blows my mind: Banks had been charged with securities fraud in 2016 and convicted in 2017, but Garnett didn't investigate the guy. He even showed up to support Banks at his sentencing hearing! Garnett ended up dropping the suit in 2019 when he and Welenken CPAs reached a private settlement, and anyway Garnett, who made about $330 million in his career and has made some forays into TV and film, should be fine. But there's a larger point here. You could be one of the biggest names in your sport and it could still happen to you.

When you're a successful professional athlete, your view of reality can become a little skewed. On the one hand, for years people have been taking care of you and giving you expert guidance in everything from your career to managing your personal life. You've learned to trust the word of authoritative coaches and mentors because they seemed to have your best interests in mind. On the other hand, you've become accustomed to being one of the best in your field. Even though that field has nothing to do with finance, it's still tempting to believe that you can bring the same level of elite skill that you brought to your chosen sport to your investment portfolio.

That's precisely where many athletes slip up, and it happens with disturbing frequency. According to Ernst & Young, pro athletes claimed nearly $600 million in fraud-related losses between 2014 and 2018. Take a wealthy young person with little financial experience and a lifetime of trusting what other people say and a shady "financial advisor" who knows what buttons to push, and you have a recipe for fraud.

The risk escalates when the athlete is busy 24-7 with competition, training, travel, team meetings, endorsements, business ventures, and family needs. It's easy for that athlete to throw a checkbook in the direction of his or her wealth manager and say, "Take care of it." When you take your eye off the ball, that's when a small minority of bad financial actors may be tempted to help themselves at your expense.

FROM THE ATHLETE
Ian Wild, Former NFL Player and Financial Advisor, on the Importance of Saving
"I got a signing bonus, and I'm pretty sure it was spent before I even got it. I went to the Canadian Football League and made a little bit of money. Once I got my chance with the Steelers,

I finally had some pretty big paydays, but that was four years later. But while it was nice to get this $50,000 check, I knew that it wouldn't last. It disappears fast. So I really planned. I put a lot into IRAs and such. Now I'm almost at a point where I don't even need to really save for retirement because I put away so much during my prime years.

"I decided to retire this past year, and the past three to four months have been pretty tough, even though I was ready for it. It's been about finding a new focus and goals. When you're training and performing at like the highest level in sports, that's really all you think about."

THE BIGGER ISSUE

However, fraud and malfeasance by financial professionals isn't the real issue I'm here to talk about. It's appalling, but it's rare. What's much more common are unwise, ill-informed or reckless—but completely legal—financial decisions made by athletes and their financial teams. I'm talking about things like investments in flawed businesses, portfolios with too much or too little risk, excessive purchases, and botched tax planning. Those cause much more pain and loss for pro athletes.

Remember, you're not just an athlete. You're a brand and a business. If you want to enjoy a fruitful career and beyond, you need to start acting like a CEO. While it's crucial for every professional athlete to build a team of professionals, it's just as important that you become reasonably conversant in this area. You don't have to study for months to earn your license to sell securities or go back to college to earn your MBA (though there are athletes who have done both), but you *should* become involved in every aspect of your finances and knowledgeable enough to know the right questions. That's why I created my Financial Literacy for Athletes educational video series. Access it at WealthLit101.com, and start learning what you need to know.

Of course, there are no "one-size-fits-all" financial plans and solutions. The challenges and opportunities that come with a professional sports career will be different depending on the kind of career you've had and the money you've made. So let's look at the challenges and opportunities that each of our five types of athletes will face.

THE UP-AND-COMER

- *Young*
- *Inexperienced*
- *Has played for fewer than than three years or undrafted*

When I speak to young professionals just starting out in careers like law or business, I give them all the same piece of advice: *Start early*. For instance, when we're talking about investing in a qualified retirement account like an IRA or 401(k), the earlier you begin setting aside money, the better because compounding has more time to work for your benefit. In this context it's important to start thinking about your financial stability and long-term prosperity even if you haven't been drafted yet (if you're in a sport with a draft) or if you're in the first few years of your career and maybe not yet making the big bucks.

In my first book, *Walk Away Wealthy*, the most important advice I gave to business owners thinking about selling their companies was to "plan for the exit from the beginning." In other words, while your business is young, you should be doing the smart things that will enable you to sell it for the highest possible price in twenty years: building a diverse customer base, developing a clear, comprehensive operations manual, and making sure the company can run without your hands-on involvement. I'd give the same advice to any pro athlete:

As early as you can, start making plans for when you're no longer playing.

"Right toward the end of my career, I started thinking, 'Wow, okay. The end of my career is coming up,'" said Mike Golic. "But I had a connection because of a piece I did on [quarterback] Randall Cunningham's show, so I got in touch with ESPN and they were like, 'When you're done, you want to start doing games?' I had never thought of that. Luckily, I kind of fell into it. As they say, the rest is history. I started off doing college games, and when the Jacksonville Jaguars came in the league in 1995, I was their first preseason TV color guy, and then it just kind of all rolled from there to where it is now."

Here are some of the unique situations the young up-and-comer might face, both good and potentially problematic:

Opportunities

- **The Draft.** You may be looking at a professional draft, which could affect your early earnings, depending on what sport you play and where you're drafted. If you are and you don't have a sports agent, this is the time to interview several, check their references and reputations, and choose someone who can help you get the best draft result possible, whether that's a high draft position, a great signing bonus, or both.

- **The Team You Want.** If you're just starting out, you probably don't have your financial team yet: CPA, financial advisor, tax preparer, and so on. Good. That means you're not trudging uphill against the weight of past mistakes. You can build your team from scratch, taking advantage of referrals and advice from the people who know best: coaches, agents, and financially stable teammates. Ideally, your financial team should be with you during your career and far beyond, so take the time to do this right.

- **Your Brand.** As a younger player, you're already aware of the incredible power of social media and the internet; they can make celebrities in a few hours, but they can also break them. Think of Tim Tebow. The guy came out of the University of Florida with two NCAA championships in his back pocket, flopped with the Denver Broncos, and then decided to try baseball before flopping with the New York Mets. But because he led with his Christian faith and worked social media like a boss, he's become a sensation regardless, with a bestselling book, a broadcasting career, and work as an actor, producer, speaker, and brand ambassador. As I am writing this, he has 4.5 million followers on Twitter and 2.5 million on Instagram. If that's failure, I'll take it.

Tebow has done an amazing job building his brand, and as a young player, you can do the same, and you should. Early in your career, you're fresh and unknown, without (hopefully) the negative baggage that older players can sometimes have after years of partying, blowing up at reporters and game officials, or rocky marriages. Your brand is what you stand for in the eyes of fans and the media, and when you're a young player, you get to decide what that brand is. But you have to make good, smart choices. If you don't, even a sterling brand can tarnish fast.

Just look at NFL wideout Antonio Brown for the other extreme. Early in his career with the Pittsburgh Steelers, he was one of the hottest wide receivers in the game, a sure superstar and multimillionaire. Then, after multiple run-ins with the law, accusations of everything from domestic violence to burglary, decisions to retire and then unretire, and a suspension for part of the 2020 season, his brand was shredded.

Your brand lives on long after you've exited the locker room for the last time, so good or bad, it will affect your future earning power. We're in the age of internet-branded athletes, and if you're taking charge of your online brand and developing it in a smart, strategic way, you can really cash in. Josh Hoffman, Chief Strategy Officer of the Institute for Athlete Branding and Marketing, writes, "For athletes who have a strong internet-driven brand—a large, engaged, ever-growing following and resounding influence over their fanbase—this shift in advertising is a major opportunity to scale marketing earnings, as well as to double, triple or, dare I say, 10x the earnings they would otherwise make."

- **Smart Financial Habits**. Much of the financial pain that professional athletes experience doesn't come from bad advisors. It's self-inflicted. They cause their own misery with reckless overspending, investing in a friend's questionable business, not paying taxes, and so on. It's stupid and unnecessary. Now is the time to work with your financial team and lay down some rules for yourself. Live on a budget. Save or invest a set amount of your income. Auto-pay your debts so you don't incur late fees. Designate a "bad guy" with the power to say no to loans to buddies and dumb spending decisions. The time to start developing disciplined financial habits that will serve you well for a lifetime is right now, before you have big expenses and bigger expectations.

- **Time to Pivot.** Every athlete wants a twenty-year career that earns him $100 million. But things don't usually work out that way. Most pro careers in any sport only last a few years; most athletes aren't stars. But if you were to play for two or three years and decide either that you couldn't compete at the level you desire or that the sport just wasn't for you, you'd still have time to pivot to something else— coaching, broadcasting, business, or what have you. That's a lot easier to do when you're twenty-six than when you're thirty-six.

- **High Energy.** You're young, healthy, and full of energy. Great. Use it to make yourself the best player you can be. Use it to become indispensable to your team—a super-utility man in baseball, a defensive specialist in basketball, or maybe something like an MMA striker known for knockouts. This goes back to the basic principle I've already hit on: most pro athletes aren't superstars, so you have to do whatever you can to stay relevant in your sport and make the best living you can for as long as you can.

You should also use your energy to develop your side hustle, whether that's business, real estate, acting, broadcasting, or something else. *This is critical!* You must have at least one side hustle while you're playing because it will probably become your leading source of income when you're retired. No matter what, you won't play your sport forever, so lay the groundwork for your future now.

Challenges

- **Inexperience.** If you've never had money, you don't know your options. As a young player, you don't know what you don't know, but know this: you need help. Early in your career, especially if you're fortunate enough to get a big signing bonus, is when you'll make your biggest financial mistakes out of ignorance and recklessness.

- **Predators.** Even if you don't make millions, people will assume you do because that's the pro athlete stereotype. You might become a target for fraudsters and scammers, and you might find friends, family members, and even old high school teammates coming to you with their hands out. Do yourself a favor and say no to everyone until you have a financial team to say no and enforce discipline.

- **Unpredictable Career Path and Income.** At this point you have no idea how long your career will be or how much you'll earn, which makes it difficult to plan for the long term. My advice is to plan as if each year of your career is the last year until—if you're lucky enough to do this—you sign a guaranteed long-term team, sponsorship, or endorsement contract that locks in several years of predictable income.

- **You're Unknown.** It's tough to land endorsement deals and the like when nobody knows who you are. Having a strong social media presence can help, as I mentioned earlier, but even if you have that, you're going to have to hustle to get even a sniff of the deals that the bigger names get. Be patient, keep playing, build your brand, and build your team. Deals will come.

- **Few Assets.** You're not making max contract dollars yet, so you've got less to work with. You can save, but you may have to put off some bigger purchases. That's all right. Do what you can with what you have and—do I have to say it again?—start early.

KNOW THE SCORE
What NFL Draft Money Looks Like

There are a lot of misconceptions about the kind of money NFL draft picks get, especially guys drafted after the first round. Believe me, the numbers drop off *fast* after round one. Courtesy of Football Next Level:

2019 NFL DRAFT ANALYSIS—
AVERAGE GUARANTEED DOLLARS BY ROUND

First Round—$16,939,370

Second Round—$3,786,853

Third Round—$946,211

Fourth Round—$692,925

Fifth Round—$301,369

Sixth Round—$161,745

Seventh Round—$88,795

These numbers include base salary, signing, roster, and option bonuses that are guaranteed

UNDRAFTED FREE AGENTS

Average signing bonus: $5,000
2020 rookie minimum salary: $610,000
Weekly pay if on fifty-three man roster: $35,882
2020 practice squad weekly pay: $8,400 ($142,800 if on all
seventeen weeks)
Players who are drafted sign four-year contracts
Players who are not drafted sign three-year contracts
An undrafted contact done in 2020 would be three years with no signing bonus for $2,285,000 (nothing guaranteed)

THE RISING STAR

- *At least three years of professional experience*
- *Income anywhere from league average to high rent*
- *Financial team is in place*

This is any pro athlete who is expecting his or her earning power to dramatically increase, either through a big contract, larger prize purses, more desirable endorsements, or some combo of all of them. You're upwardly mobile with high upside potential. Deals are floating around, your agent is talking big numbers, and things are up in the air. You don't know how much you're going to earn or, very possibly, where you're going to play next. It's both an exciting and nerve-wracking time in your life when you have the chance to make life-changing money and set up a prosperous future by making some good decisions.

Opportunities

- **Freedom.** You have the potential to earn more, play where you want, and pursue the opportunities you want. You can shoot for the highest salary you think you can command and be in control of your own career, maybe for the first time.

- **Guaranteed Money.** If you're in position to sign a contract with a team, you'll have guaranteed income. Same if you sign a guaranteed contract as an endorser or brand ambassador. That's money in the bank, which means you can relax a little. If it's a big number or a long contract, perhaps you can do some of the things you've always wanted to do, like pay off your parents' house or invest in a Silicon Valley start-up.

- For example, take defensive end Joey Bosa of the Los Angeles Chargers. In 2020, he signed an eye-popping contract extension paying him $135 million over five years with $78 million of it fully guaranteed at signing. When you have that kind of security, the sky's the limit.

- **Negotiating Power.** Not all pro athletes have negotiating power. For example, NFL players have "slots" that determine their salary range for each position based on how many years of experience they have. But for other sports, you can negotiate with multiple teams or sponsors to try to come to the best deal possible. That's leverage you don't have when you're a younger player.

- **Forging Long-Term Relationships.** One of the best things about being a more experienced player with staying power in your sport is that you can start putting down roots. Not just with your family but also in the business community. You can invest the time in building your local network and taking some of the essential steps toward building multiple secondary streams of income, such as buying real estate or investing in regional franchises that you like.

Challenges

- **Unpredictability.** Of course, the downside to the freedom and flexibility of being a free agent or seeking your next big deal is that not knowing how much you'll earn or where you'll play makes it difficult to make plans, especially if you have a family. You might have an idea of your likely salary range, but until the ink is dry, that's just a guess. That's why former NFL safety Matt Bowen wrote, "That's the reality of free agency . . . most players won't bring in multiyear deals with massive signing bonuses . . . most will be waiting around, like I did. Those low-to-midtier free agents, who make up the majority of the talent pool, will be waiting for a phone call and a new deal."

  Plus, there's the reality that you could land a big contract or start making big money, make commitments based on your healthier finances (like buying a home), and then suffer a reversal. Portland Trail Blazers star Brandon Roy signed a max dollar contract, but in 2011 a degenerative knee condition forced him to retire. He's coaching now, but I'll guarantee you his income is a lot lower than when he was playing.

- **Poor Representation.** When you're trying to land a new deal with your current team or a new team or trying to close a sponsorship deal, you're completely dependent on your sports agent. He (or she) is the one calling general managers and team executives and handling the negotiations. If you have incompetent representation, it could cost you millions of dollars. That's why smart players get involved in negotiations and never agree to a contract based solely on their agent's say-so. It's important to have checks and balances. To quote the noted philosopher Kanye West, "No one man should have all that power."

- **Cash Flow.** Former NFL safety Andre Hal has confirmed what you probably already know. "Everybody thinks you're rich," he has said, talking about the people who come running as soon as an athlete makes the pros. The fact is, even after you sign a decent free agent contract, you're not instantly rolling in cash like Scrooge McDuck.

Let's go back to free agency as an example. The process varies from sport to sport. For example, the NFL has restricted and unrestricted free agency. Once their contracts expire, unrestricted free agents can test the open market and negotiate with any team. Restricted free agents, on the other hand, are players with three years of service who become eligible to receive one-year qualifying offers. Major League Baseball has the qualifying offer system, in which players are offered a one-year contract for a league-determined amount. If the player declines, the team gets draft compensation when the player signs elsewhere. It's all very complicated, but the basics are roughly the same.

Generally, in any team sport, a player must put in a minimum amount of service time to be eligible for free agency. Once that threshold is reached, the player and his agent navigate different free agent designations—restricted, unrestricted, undrafted—and issues like salary caps and qualifying offers, and the agent can begin fielding offers from other teams as well as from the player's original team. As those offers come in, the agent and player weigh the various factors—salary, bonuses, deferred money, the location of the team and the commercial opportunities in that city, tax laws in different places—and choose a final winner.

The thing many new free agents don't understand is that if you sign a four-year contract for $12 million, you don't get a check in the mail for $12 million. First of all, you're only getting $3 million of that salary per year. Second, you don't get it all at once. If you're playing in the NFL, you'll get seventeen checks, one for each game of the season. Taxes will be taken out of those checks, and those taxes can vary depending on where you earned the money because pro athletes have to pay taxes for each city and state where they play—the famous "jock tax."

Let's say that on average taxes equal 35 percent of your total earnings for each week in the NFL. That means you're getting seventeen after-tax payments averaging $114,705. The other thirty-five weeks of the year, unless you have another job or an endorsement deal, you're earning $0. If you don't manage your spending wisely, you're going to run into some serious cash flow issues or rack up a lot of debt.

- **Higher Expenses.** Since free agency comes later in careers, by the time athletes are signing that multiyear contract, many have more expenses: a family, a mortgage, maybe child support, care for aging parents, and so on. Even if you have a higher income, it can be consumed pretty quickly by higher costs.

THE SOLID VETERAN

- *Five-plus years of experience*
- *May have played for multiple teams or in multiple leagues*
- *Solid but not elite earning power*
- *Solid relationships with teammates, executives, staff, press*

You're not a superstar, but you've been talented and hardworking enough to stick around in your sport for five, six, maybe even seven years and make pretty good money. You might be a long snapper, a three-point specialist, a left-handed reliever, or a solid second-tier PGA pro, and by being willing to move around and be versatile, you've built a nice career. Now you're midway through it, and it's become obvious that you're never going to make Cam Newton, Bryce Harper, or Rory McIlroy money. That's no problem, as long as you're smart.

Opportunities

- **Pension Vesting.** If you're an MLB player and you play for ten full seasons, you're fully vested in the league's pension program. If you start drawing your pension at forty-five, you'll get around $68,000 a year, but if you wait until age sixty-two, you could pull $220,000 per year.

Bridging that seventeen-year gap could make you an extra $150,000 a year, which is not chump change.

If you manage to stick in the NBA for three years, you could earn at least $56,988 per year from your pension, up to a ceiling of $195,000 for eleven-year vets. Plus, the league will match a player's contributions to the league-sponsored 401(k) by—I am not making this up—*140 percent*. So for every $10,000 you contribute to your retirement account, the NBA puts in $14,000. Top that, corporate America.

So yeah, it's great to stick around long enough to fully vest in a pension program. (Of course, there's also the advantage of staying in your sport for twelve, thirteen, or fourteen years and continuing to make seven figures a year.) The NFL, NHL, and even the PGA have one, and over the years it's helped save a lot of retired players from poverty. That said, while the pension is a nice bit of icing on the cake, it's not something you should rely on for your entire retirement income, any more than a retired corporate executive should rely on Social Security. It's a bonus, but you need a lot more money to live on.

- **Employable Knowledge.** Longtime players in any sport are prime candidates to become coaches. Why? Because one of the reasons you've hung on is your knowledge of the game. You're smart and savvy. You know how to take care of your body. That makes you a potentially great fit for a gig as a coach, trainer, or even a team broadcaster or analyst.

- **Network.** You've been around the game for a while, and if you're a good guy or gal and well-liked, you've probably built up a wide network of business contacts, media professionals, entertainment figures, agents, lawyers, and the like. You attend events like Leveraging the Athlete Platform, an annual event put on by sports and entertainment agency Sports Biz Group, where athletes learn how to turn the prestige and visibility of being a pro athlete into business opportunities.

- **Established Portfolio.** You've hung around long enough to make a few million dollars, and if you've been smart with it, you've been investing. Not just stocks and mutual funds but also private equity, venture capital funds, start-ups, and franchises. You've got a mature portfolio and a comprehensive plan for investing, taxes, insurance, retirement, and more.

Challenges

- **Being Cut.** At this stage of your career, while you might be a useful player, you're probably also somewhat expendable. Perhaps your role could be filled by a younger, cheaper player or your skills are beginning to decline, but the fact is that there's a chance that any season could be your last. When the end comes, it almost always comes suddenly and with a frightening drop in income.

- **Complacency and Ignorance.** If you've been in the game for a while, you probably have an established routine, a trusted team, and a financial strategy. Great. But good financial plans evolve over time, and if you aren't driving your financial team to constantly adjust your plan for changing times and your changing career, you could be losing money. Ignorance of financial trends is just as dangerous. It's your money, so you have some responsibility for keeping up on changes in the stock and bond market, the real estate market, tax laws, and much more.

    Keep in mind that I am not suggesting you have to become an expert in finances and investing. However, if you're completely oblivious, you're asking for trouble—or fraud. It's smart to become educated in the basics, which is why I'm going to take another opportunity to pump my Financial Literacy for Athletes video program at WealthLit101.com. For $99, I'll give you a rock-solid grounding in the essentials you need to know. Think of it as a financial self-defense course.

- **Less Corporate Appeal.** Big brands generally want superstars to be their brand ambassadors, and we've already established that you're not a superstar. If you've worked hard to create goodwill in your local market like Justin Turner of the Los Angeles Dodgers, you can still land some lucrative local endorsements and sponsorships. But with the "journeyman" label attached to you, you're more apt to be representing smaller regional brands that don't pay as much.

THE SUNSETTING VETERAN

- *Performance is declining*
- *Lengthy career of seven-plus years*
- *Most likely a year or two from retirement or release*
- *Established family and home*
- *Actively looking at post-play career options*

This is the hardest period for many professional athletes. For ten years or more, your sport is all you've known. It's defined your world and your identity. It's given you your friends and your social circle. And it's enabled you to make a living that puts you in the top 1 percent of the population. And now that's all about to end, suddenly, with no fanfare, as with the catcher from the movie *Major League*, Jake Taylor.

As NBA Hall of Famer Kareem Abdul-Jabbar wrote in *The Guardian*, "For athletes who have managed to beat the odds and stay in the sports spotlight for many years, our final bow can feel a little too final . . . many . . . with double-digit years in the gladiatorial arena are relatively young when we retire, usually in our thirties or forties. Which is when we ask ourselves the existential question: who am I now?"

Many athletes struggle with the sudden end of what's been the center of their lives. A BBC survey of retired athletes found that half had experienced concerns about their mental or emotional health since retirement. Having a strong financial plan, not to mention plans for business ventures and other activities, can help.

Opportunities

- **Time.** If your career is drawing to a close, you can spend less time on physical training, drills, and other activities than you did when you were a younger player. You can spend less time traveling, hanging with teammates, and living the lifestyle of an athlete and more time working on your all-important side hustle (for instance, buying Wendy's franchises), getting your financial and business affairs organized, and pursuing possible opportunities in media, broadcasting, or coaching.

- **Assets.** If you've invested steadily and wisely since you began your career, you should have more financial assets to use for new ventures as your playing days end. For example, if you were able to invest just $100,000 per year in the stock market, with a diversified portfolio, you could reasonably expect an average annualized return of about 7 percent. If you got that kind of return for a ten-year playing career, you would end up with about $1.4 million—a substantial amount you could use to continue investing in the markets, start a business, develop a product line, or buy a franchise.

- **Retirement Programs.** Practically every major sport, even individual sports like golf, has its own retirement program for its players. Gone are the days when retired professional athletes quickly fell into poverty because they had no marketable skills; you have to mismanage your life pretty terribly, like Mike Tyson or Evander Holyfield, to wind up in debt and broke these days. Even if you never made huge money, the PGA, Major League Soccer, the Association of Tennis Professionals (ATP) tour, the WNBA, certainly the heavy hitters like the NFL, NBA, NHL, and MLB—everyone has a 401(k) or pension program. Put in the minimum years (and in the case of the 401(k), make the required contributions) and you're in.

- **Post-career Training.** There are numerous training and educational programs designed to help retired pro athletes transition to the next stage of their lives with minimal financial disruption. Many are run by retired athletes, who know that leaving behind years of camaraderie, adrenaline, challenge, and competition, not to mention physical activity and a big paycheck, can leave athletes feeling lost and rudderless. From the Professional Athlete's Entrepreneur Network (PAEN) to in-house training programs focused on pro athletes at companies like Ernst & Young to companies like NexGoal Recruiting, which pairs former athletes with corporate employers seeking retired competitors, you can take advantage of endless resources designed to help you move to the next stage of your life and leverage the prestige, visibility, and brand appeal that comes with being an athlete.

Challenges

- **Plummeting Income.** As I've already made depressingly clear, once you retire, it's a near-certainty that your income will fall off a cliff. This doesn't have to be a traumatic time; we don't live in the era when athletes made so little money playing that they needed full-time jobs in the off-season to make ends meet, like the legendary story of Yankees great Yogi Berra waiting tables at Ruggeri's Italian restaurant in Saint Louis in the 1950s. But it is devastating for athletes who aren't prepared for the income falloff or who can't dial back their lavish spending habits.

- **Depression.** There's an old saying that goes, "The leading cause of death among older Americans is retirement." Meaning, losing a sense of purpose and not having a place to be each day leads to depression and illness. That's certainly true for retired pro athletes. Many athletes from a wide range of sports have spoken openly about their struggles adapting to "civilian" life. Ex–pro basketball player and entrepreneur Malcolm Lemmons, founder of Players Point, a company that helps athletes build their personal brands beyond sports, writes about the life of the athlete:

You begin to love the adrenaline rush and it becomes a part of your everyday life. It becomes routine and as people, we all find comfort in routine and habit. Transitioning into a "nonathlete" breaks that routine. It creates a sense of unfamiliarity and discomfort which leads to confusion and questioning your self-worth. For some athletes, this is usually what leads to depression in life after sports. Athletes lose their sense of being and purpose, and when you're accustomed to being "someone" for so long, it's really hard to be someone else.

- **Diminishing Skills.** The thing is, while your athleticism and playing skills will diminish, your brand doesn't have to. It's more important than your ability to throw a ninety-eight mile-per-hour fastball or fire a wicked backhand. Again, take Conor McGregor. He's had some minor run-ins with the police and courts and been accused of some other transgressions, but that comes with being world-famous. He's also built his side hustles, including about $8 million in annual endorsement income from companies like Reebok and Anheuser-Busch, his own fashion line, and the Proper No. Twelve Irish whiskey line. He knows that anyone's body can only take punishment for so long, and he's leveraging his brand for the day when his body taps out.

- **Lack of Practical Experience.** Suppose you've spent twenty years, from high school to your midthirties, doing one thing and training to become great at that one thing. Suddenly you're dropped, dazed and blinking, in the world of the rest of us and told, "Okay, find employment." That's not just disorienting, it's unrealistic. Sure, if you managed to save millions of dollars during your career, you might not need to work or you might have all the time you need to find your next gig. But that's not most retired athletes. Most need to earn a living after playing, and if you have no marketable skills and no experience, that's going to be a challenge. That's why many retired pros either take steps during their careers to move into areas like broadcasting or return to what they know as coaches or front office personnel.

THE SOLOIST

- *You're essentially an independent contractor*
- *You've worked hard to compete in a sport like cycling, tennis, golf, swimming, or mixed martial arts*
- *A substantial portion of your earnings come from sponsorships and endorsements*
- *You might not have a league retirement plan as a safety net*

What makes the life of a solo athlete so challenging is that your income is largely based on winning: you need to make the cut in a PGA tournament or finish in the money in a race in order to get paid. So if your performance slips because of age or injury, your income can go south like a goose in winter. This variation on athletic life comes with financial opportunities and challenges unlike those of team athletes.

Opportunities

- **Flexibility.** Because you're probably not affiliated with a team, you have greater flexibility to pursue all manner of business and professional opportunities, from branded products to small business ventures to brand ambassadorships. You don't have a front office telling you what you can and can't do.

- **Expanded Sponsorships.** Many individual sports are known for the profusion of sponsor logos on their participants. Golf is well-known for this, but tennis, NASCAR, pro cycling, and pro triathlon are also filled with athletes who look like walking billboards. That's not a criticism; if you have the popularity, success, and business savvy to land sponsors and augment your income, that's earned money.

Challenges

- **No Guaranteed Income.** The big downside to a purse-based income stream is that you're like any independent contractor: if you don't work and don't perform, you don't get paid.

   Jim Caple, an ESPN reporter, wrote about this in a great piece about life on the fringes of pro golf. About PGA star Dustin Johnson and one of his college teammates, another pro named Zack Byrd, Caple wrote, "After golfing together three years at Coastal Carolina University, where Byrd still holds the school record for lowest score, the two each played the 2011 US Open. Johnson made $76,455 for finishing twenty-third. Byrd missed the cut and received $2,000, which didn't cover his expenses for the week. Their career earnings gap is even wider. While Johnson has made a fortune, Byrd estimates his seven-year pro earnings at probably under $250,000, possibly less than his expenses have been."

   That's a tough way to live.

- **No Safety Net.** Without a team or league structure behind you, not only might you lack a formal retirement program, but you probably also don't have a labor union to advocate for you when it comes to contracts, benefits, and the like. You're on your own.

- **High Expenses.** One of the great luxuries of playing for a team in a major sports league is that whether you're suiting up for MLB, the

WNBA, or MLS, your team is picking up the bill. Travel costs, hotels, trainers, equipment—you don't have to worry about those expenses. That's not the case if you're a soloist as a tennis player, marathoner, or skater. All those expenses fall on you, which could mean hundreds of thousands of dollars out of your pocket each year.

TIME-OUT

Expert guidance and legal counsel can help protect your rights as an amateur. For years the NCAA did not allow its athletes to receive any sort of payment from agents, sponsors, or other entities for fear they would be influenced by the money— which, since many college athletes are broke, was probably a fair assumption. Now the NCAA is finally allowing collegiate stars to profit from the use of their names, images, and likenesses (NIL) on things like jerseys and video games. And in April of 2020, the NCAA Board of Governors agreed to allow student-athletes to "receive compensation for third-party endorsements both related to and separate from athletics," as well as for other student-athlete opportunities, like social media and personal appearances.

That's great, but it doesn't mean college athletics is a free-for-all. The NCAA still bans name, image, and likeness activities that could be considered "pay for play," doesn't allow the athlete's school or conference to be involved in these for-profit activities, and still tightly regulates the activities of agents and advisors. Also, an athlete's name, image, and likeness cannot be used for recruiting by schools or boosters.

Bottom line, you've still got to be careful. In 2019, James Wiseman, a top recruit and possible number-one NBA draft pick at the University of Memphis, was ruled ineligible by the NCAA because of his connection to Memphis head coach and former NBA star Penny Hardaway, who had been a booster of Wiseman's. He ended up dropping out of school and being drafted number two in November of 2020 by the Golden State Warriors. In other words, this issue is complex, which is why you need experts in your corner to make sure you don't end up sanctioned or disqualified from play.

ALL SITUATIONS HAVE THE SAME SOLUTION

As we've seen from the many, many stories of multimillionaire pro athletes who wind up broke and bankrupt, even making huge money in your sport doesn't solve all your financial problems. In fact, it can even lead to new ones. But whatever situation you're in—high-ticket star, working ballplayer, free agent, young, nearing retirement—the solution is always the same: *building a top-flight Board of Directors made of people you can trust.* These are the people who will manage your AES and run your business affairs—your chief marketing officer (CMO), chief financial officer (CFO), and chief operating officer (COO).

Let's begin with your sports agent, your CMO. This was the first professional outside of your sport whom you likely had contact with, and he's had your back in contract and sponsor negotiations ever since. Your agent should be a solid resource for building your championship financial squad because he may have relationships with many of the specialists you'll need, especially if he works for a large agency. But even if your agent doesn't have those relationships, you can ask former teammates, coaches, and front office staff for referrals. They've seen it all, and they know who can and can't be trusted. A money-savvy family member or longtime family attorney could also be a good resource. Your pro league, if you're part of one, may also have recommendations and guidelines for hiring financial pros.

Here's the lineup you'll need to put together (apart from your sports agent, whom I'm going to assume you already have):

- **Leadoff.** The linchpin of this lineup will be your financial advisor, your CFO, the quarterback of your financial life. This will be a licensed professional who develops and manages financial portfolios and comprehensive investment, financial, and tax strategies for clients. I recommend that this person be a CERTIFIED FINANCIAL PLANNER™ professional, or CFP®, because CFPs® are subject to the strictest regulation and have to meet the most rigorous qualifications to practice.

- **Batting second.** Even before you start to build a mini-empire of businesses, appearances, books, and sponsorships, you'll want a **business manager** to keep your socks pulled up and your shoes tied. This is your COO, the person who keeps your life running smoothly. A dedicated business manager will handle everything from contracts and bills to appointments and correspondence and can even double as a personal assistant.

- **Batting third.** You'll also want a **tax specialist**—a certified public accountant (CPA), an Enrolled Agent, or even an attorney with an advanced degree in taxation. This will be your point person for tax planning as well as preparing your tax return and ensuring that federal, state, and local taxes are paid. Ideally, find someone with experience in dealing with the unique tax situations affecting pro athletes or someone with experience in *forensic accounting*, an investigative form of accounting commonly used as part of legal or tax disputes.

- **Cleanup.** Early in your career, you may not need an **attorney** on retainer, and you possibly can't afford one, but you should still know one you can call. Later on, if you stick in your sport and start earning more and building a higher profile, having your own go-to legal eagle, even if it's someone from your agent's office, is vital. With success, you could see everything from business proposals and book deals to (unfortunately) litigation and illegal use of your name and likeness.

You'll want a good lawyer on hand to help things run smoothly. Think of the fees as insurance for your brand and reputation.

- **Utility player**. A **Controller** to handle your day-to-day finances. This will be the person who keeps track of your regular spending, expenses, banking activity, estimated tax payments, and the like, as well as record-keeping.

- **Pinch hitter.** I hope you don't need a **security specialist**, but if you become well-known and successful, it's a good idea to have somebody on call. Today, personal security can include physical security, cybersecurity, and protection of information like your Social Security and credit card numbers. Here, prevention is everything.

Your Board of Directors will be there to look after your interests during contract negotiations as well as sponsorship and endorsement negotiations. They'll help you manage your investments, vet new investment opportunities, set up bank and brokerage accounts, prepare and file your taxes, and create a personal budget and savings plan. They'll also assist you with keeping your information secure, keeping unsavory people out of your life, and preventing damage from bad PR. In other words, they're around to make sure you have every opportunity to turn your talent and years of hard work into a prosperous, enjoyable life— both while you're still playing and after you're done. Putting that team in place as soon as possible should be one of your highest priorities.

What about your team or league? Won't they advise you? Probably, but that advice will typically be general—guidelines, warnings, resources. There's nothing wrong with that, but it's no substitute for personalized solutions. The exception is the NFL Players Association, which has a very strict process for vetting qualified advisors, including a comprehensive background check that requires explanations for everything, down to the time you put a plastic bottle in the trash can instead of recycle bin. I asked Fred Claire, who served as general manager for the Los Angeles Dodgers from 1987–1997, about team advice:

> Our philosophy was to educate our players, and in spring training, when we had all of our players together, we would bring in a financial advisor. We would identify the people who we knew had great reputations, great histories, and who would really serve our players from an educational standpoint.
>
> For me, I tried to build good relationships with the players and build a sense of trust. I can remember Orel Hershiser, whom I signed to a contract that made him the highest paid player in the game at the time, coming to me and saying, "Fred, I'm looking to buy a home in Pasadena, and I know you live in Pasadena, would you give me guidance or introduce me to a person in real estate?" Which I did. That exemplified what I tried to convey to the player, which was: "We care about you beyond what you're doing on the field."

Fred Claire is a class act. However, not all GMs and teams show the same kind of personal care for their players, which is why you need a team that's looking out for *your* interests. Let's move on to the next chapter and look at exactly how to do that.

OVERTIME

Retired players' associations are incredibly valuable assets for players who have hung 'em up and are trying to make the most of life away from the field, court, or course. These groups work with former players on everything from adjusting to civilian life to helping them give back to the community to assisting with things like finances and medical bills. The major retired players' associations are:

• National Basketball Retired Players Association

www.legendsofbasketball.com
- NFL Retired Players Association
  www.nflretiredplayersassociation.org
- Pro Football Retired Players Association
  www.pfrpa.com
- Major League Baseball Players Alumni Association
  www.mlb.com/mlbpaa
- NHL Alumni Association
  www.nhlalumni.org

CHAPTER TWO

The Athlete Enterprise System (AES) (a.k.a. The Team That Runs "You, Inc.")

A couple of years ago, I was courting a superstar NFL player as a client. We talked at length, developed a rapport, and he eventually agreed to meet with me at his condo in Miami. So I packed my best Miami attire along with my golf clubs and flew down to Florida, and we sat down in his gorgeous living room with a view of Biscayne Bay to talk about his future.

As we did, he got a call on his cell phone and answered it. I sat and listened as the caller spent the next twenty minutes giving this multimillionaire athlete the hard sell on investing in a business he was starting. But what blew my mind (even though I didn't say anything at the time) was that this athlete sat through this whole sales pitch when he should have immediately told the caller, "This is outside my lane. You need to talk to my CFO. Here's his cell number." This superstar was wasting his time on a financial matter outside his area of expertise, something with the potential to put hundreds of thousands of dollars of his money at risk. He was too nice to just say no, which is what he should have done.

This is why sometimes you need a "bad cop" on hand to say no to people so you can stay on good terms with them. Feeling like you always have to be the "good cop" can put you in some awkward situations. I see this sort of thing—athletes' friends hitting them up to invest in their latest scheme—all the time, and it drives me crazy. This wealthy, successful athlete didn't have a gatekeeper to whom he could refer that call, someone with the business, legal, and financial savvy to determine whether it was a legitimate business opportunity or a poorly thought-out money pit—someone objective enough to say, "No thank you" so the athlete wouldn't have to.

Later, during our two days of meetings and discussions, this NFL player and I talked about that call, and he told me that he never had plans to invest in the friend's business; he was just being nice. But here's the thing: *He should never have listened to the pitch in the first place.* It wasn't his job. It was the job of one of the people helping him run his one-man pro athlete enterprise.

The call should have gone to his financial advisor, the CFO of the business. If the CFO had decided the opportunity sounded legitimate, he might have chosen to pull in the athlete's business manager and accountant for further vetting and due diligence. Only if it had turned out to be a sound investment and a good fit with the athlete's existing portfolio and brand should it have found its way across the athlete's desk. Either he didn't have a team like that in place or he did but didn't trust them. Either one was not good.

I told him all this, and I think that candor was one of the main reasons he ended up hiring me as his financial advisor and CFO. The trouble is, he's not alone. Thousands of pro athletes are flying blind financially as they earn their livings in volatile professions where their careers could end tomorrow. Many of them might be navigating the world of banking, investing, business, and taxes with nothing more than their agent and the guy from H&R Block. That's not enough. No matter which of my five athlete categories you're in, you need a Board of Directors to help you keep more of what you earn, grow those earnings over time, and build a business and a brand that will produce substantial income for you long after you've retired, so you can enjoy the lifestyle and security you deserve.

WHY YOU NEED THE AES

The right Board of Directors is about more than a financial plan. It's more than a bunch of folks who negotiate your contracts, manage your investments, and pay your taxes. The AES is an organizational chart, just like you'd find in a corporation—a decision tree of financial, business, and legal professionals who run your affairs, shield you from predators and people pitching money-losing opportunities, make sure you're saving and investing, pay your bills and your taxes, and vet opportunities with an experienced, skeptical eye. They help you make sound decisions about your money, brand, and lifestyle.

Without that guidance, some successful pro athletes have let their money go to their heads. Take pro golfer John Daly. Famous for his monster drives off the tee, he became infamous for his drinking and gambling, by his own admission drinking a fifth of Jack Daniel's each day while on the PGA Tour when he was twenty-three. Daly earned about $9 million during his career, but claims to have lost $50–60 million gambling. That's someone who needed a team to rein him in but didn't have one.

Being an active pro athlete can make you feel invincible. You're one of the best in the world at what you do, and you're making a lot of money, so you might feel like things can't go wrong. Joe McLean of Intersect Capital, whose firm manages money for athletes in the NBA, NFL, PGA, MLB, and NASCAR, says that with pro athletes "the commonality is that with great abundance comes less discipline." The reality is, there are many reasons pro athletes wind up taking it on the chin financially without professional support:

- They never learn the basics of banking, credit, debt, cash flow, the stock market, retirement accounts—anything. I've heard about athletes who didn't know how to write a check or use an ATM card. Not everything can be done with Apple Pay or Venmo!

- They invest in businesses that sound cool or that friends are starting but don't know the right questions to ask, and definitely can't read financial statements. So they throw their investment down the toilet.

- They don't understand "opportunity cost," which is when you have to choose one of multiple alternatives and lose all the potential gains from the ones you didn't choose (you could also call it the "road not taken tax"). For instance, if you lose $250,000 in a friend's dud business, that means you also lose the opportunity to invest that $250,000 in the market, which over twenty years at 7 percent interest would have become $967,421. Not only did the "opportunity" to invest in your pal's medicinal weed dispensary cost you the $250,000, but it also cost you more than $700,000 in returns.

- They feel obligated to take care of family members financially and to give money to every old buddy that comes along with his hand out. That adds up fast. Not saying no will lead to you being the one with your hand out.

- They fall into what I call the "Tomorrow Fallacy," in which athletes say to themselves, "There will always be another contract (or payday) tomorrow." Athletes who've played for a long time can get complacent and believe they'll always land another job. But one day that won't be true. Imagine being out of your profession at thirty or forty, when most people are just hitting their stride.

The solution is to think like a business and build a killer Board of Directors. That's your inner circle: three financial, business, and marketing professionals who keep you informed, reinforce smart financial behavior, execute a long-term plan, and protect you from fraud, poor choices, and down markets. This is your off-the-field team—the one that will be part of your life long after your playing days are in the rearview mirror.

Why not just one person, like a CERTIFIED FINANCIAL PLANNER? For one thing, managing the complexity of a modern pro athlete's financial life requires a broad range of disciplines in investing, taxation, accounting, law, and even technology. There's no single person who's an expert in all those fields. But the more practical reason is that your team needs internal checks and balances. Giving any single individual too much power over your finances contributes to malpractice, misconduct, and fraud. Teammates keep each other in check.

Let's look at the two tiers of professionals who make up the team that every professional athlete needs:

- **Board of Directors**. The three must-have individuals who serve as the top-line managers for everything that happens in your name, your chief marketing officer, chief financial officer, and chief operations officer. They answer directly to you and direct the activity of the rest of your team. You can't manage twenty people, but you can manage three.

- **Supporting Cast**. These are the people who you'll only need part-time or who can work for you as independent contractors or through a staffing agency. The members of your Board of Directors will usually vet them, connect you with them, and supervise them.

What about you? You're the chief executive officer, the CEO. You're still the boss. But you're hiring a Board of Directors made up of skilled experts to help you run a profitable one-person business, just like a corporate CEO does. Let's look at who they are and what they do.

TIME-OUT

Compete on the Field, Not in the Locker Room

One of the most common pitfalls for pro athletes who get into financial trouble is overspending, and one of the ways you can overspend is on personal staff because you want to look successful around your peers. Having a big personal entourage is a way of showboating for teammates and friends, showing off how successful you are. Don't try to outspend your teammates; spend your money wisely, and save or invest as much as you can. Here are some common personal staff athletes take on that are luxuries, not necessities:

POSITION	MEDIAN SALARY
Personal chef	$70,000/year
Personal trainer	$57,000/year
Butler	$50,000/year
Housekeeper	$23,000/year
Driver	$51,000/year
Private security	$100,000/year

That's a lot of cash—about $350,000 a year. You know what I'd suggest instead? Learn to cook, work out with the team, pick up your own stuff, hire a weekly maid service, and call an Uber. Either that or engage these people as needed, as independent contractors. They don't need to be on your payroll.

YOUR AGENT, YOUR CMO

Back in 2018, cornerback Richard Sherman negotiated his own contract with the NFL's San Francisco 49ers. Sherman, who was coming back from a torn Achilles tendon, signed a deal for $3 million guaranteed with $2 million roster bonus if he passed a physical early in training camp. He later told Fox Business, "I can get all the information that I need, so an agent is becoming an unnecessary commodity."

Except, not so much. It turns out that it's not unusual for players to come to camp out of shape and work their way into shape through the preseason, so Sherman had set himself up to potentially lose $2 million. Enter the NFL Players Association, which got the Niners to renegotiate the finalized contract so Sherman's physical wouldn't happen until after Week Eleven's games had been played. In other words, they dramatically improved his chances of getting that $2 million bonus.

That is why you need an agent. They tilt the odds in your favor and help steer you clear of potential pitfalls.

There are just three individuals who belong on your Board of Directors, and your agent is the first. He or she will function as your CMO, protecting and leveraging the value of your brand. If you already have an agent, then you know some of this, but in case there are some facts you're not aware of, and for athletes who don't have agents, let's get into it.

What Agents Do

A sports agent is a professional, usually with a background either in sports management or sports law, who you authorize to be your representative to the worlds of sports, finance, business, media, and entertainment. Your agent is responsible for negotiating contract terms with your existing team, fielding offers from other teams, and finding and negotiating endorsement, sponsorship, and brand ambassadorship deals, all while managing your relationship with your team or league. They might also work to find you opportunities in television, film, or broadcasting (though a talent agent might also fill that role) and work with your publicist to manage your public image and press coverage. For most pro athletes, their sports agent is their closest professional ally who's not a teammate or coach.

However, the best agents go beyond simply trying to get their players the most money; they work to make sure their clients are in a position to lead happy, prosperous, and meaningful lives. Writing in *Forbes*, superagent Leigh Steinberg (the model for Tom Cruise's character in the film *Jerry Maguire*) said, "There is an obligation to truly understand a young man or woman's greatest hopes and dreams and most limiting apprehensions and fears. This process can be initiated by asking an athlete to be internally introspective and evaluate their own goals and priorities."

In other words, the ideal sports agent should understand what you want from your career, respect those desires, and work to help you build the best career and life possible. Do you want to play near your family? Do charitable work? Invest for after retirement? Win a championship? Those are all variables that a good agent should factor into the equation of where you'll play, whom you'll play for, and the terms of your contract. Your agent should be just as interested in keeping you healthy and free from injury and preparing you for a rewarding postretirement career in broadcasting, business, or speaking as he is in signing you to big deals and collecting his commission.

The agent-client relationship looks a little different if you're an individual athlete like a golfer or boxer. Here your agent isn't negotiating with a team, but might be negotiating prize purses, appearance fees, and endorsement deals.

How Your Agent Impacts Your Finances

Your agent's work will shape your income stream for a great deal of your playing career. His negotiations will have a lot to do with how much you get in salary, bonuses, endorsement and sponsorship income, and related activities like being a guest broadcaster. His skill at landing you the right deals will dramatically affect your earnings.

However, your agent will impact your finances in other, more indirect ways. For example, if you play a team sport, the city you play in can affect your endorsement opportunities and visibility in the press, which translate into dollars. Your agent should be keeping that in mind, careful to balance your commercial prospects with your personal desires (not every athlete wants to play in New York or LA). Also, as one of the people you trust the most, your agent should be an advisor and sounding board who can guide you regarding life choices, behavior, and character. Sponsors and brands want spokespeople of good character who will represent their brands well, not embarrass them. So do teams. Brandon Averill, CFP®, a former minor league baseball player who's now a Southern California wealth manager working largely with current and former MLB players, explains:

> We have a client, a former major leaguer, an obscure name that most people probably wouldn't know, Darnell McDonald. He might've only gotten four or five years of MLB of service time, but everybody loves "D-Mac." He's just a solid human being. When his career was over, he got a job with the Cubs, and while he brings a lot of value from a baseball standpoint, I know that's also because of his relationship with the CEO and the fact that he respects D-Mac and wants him around.
>
> I've got numerous examples of that. You see it every year at the winter meetings, lots of players roaming the lobby looking for jobs, and . . . and it's sad, frankly. You can tell that some of them did some things during their career, and they didn't take it seriously, and now they're paying a price.

If you doubt that character can impact your wallet, think back to Darryl Strawberry and Dwight "Doc" Gooden of the New York Mets. Back in the mid-1980s, they *owned* New York as the marquee players on what was the city's glamour team at the time. But the hard-partying life sucked them in, and they both wound up derailed by cocaine abuse, which curtailed what could have been Hall of Fame careers and instead left them scrambling for contracts with multiple teams. Your agent's job is to help you be the most valuable and most marketable version of yourself.

Your agent is also an expense. Like any other agent, your sports agent is paid a commission, a percentage of your pretax playing salary and bonuses. The professional leagues typically put a cap on the commissions agents can collect. Agents representing NFL players can take no more than 3 percent of a client's playing contract, while NBA agent commissions are capped at 4 percent. Scott Boras, the MLB superagent, gets 5 percent. So you get the range. An agent will also earn between 10 and 20 percent of your pretax endorsement fees.

Finding the Right Agent

Most of the time, the most reliable way to find a quality service provider is to get referrals from colleagues, and a sports agent is no exception. If you don't already have one, you probably know teammates or fellow competitors who do. Ask for recommendations from people you trust. Maybe a mentor or coach. Some other things to keep in mind as you consider sports agents:

- While large sports agencies like Boras Corp., Relativity Sports, and Wasserman Media Group are not the only options, working with a big agency may have its advantages. Your agent will have been vetted by the agency, so you can be confident he or she is competent and ethical. Also, large agencies often have other divisions that can connect you with opportunities in areas like entertainment, broadcasting, and entrepreneurship.

- Your agent doesn't have to have a law degree, but legal training certainly comes in handy when dealing with contracts. Consider agents with backgrounds in sports law. Sports law is a specialized degree at universities like Marquette and the University of Miami.

- The major professional sports leagues and associations (along with the NCAA) all certify sports agents. In most cases, to be certified, an agent must have at least a bachelor's degree, pass an exam and a background check, and pay a fee. Avoid agents who are not certified by the league or association governing your sport.

- There is no single governing association for sports agents. Back in 2012, a group called the National Association of Sports Agents & Athlete Representatives announced its formation, but it never went anywhere. There is the Black Sports Agents Association (www.blacksportsagents.com) and the Sports Lawyers Association (www.sportslaw.org), which could offer suggestions about agents.

- A prospective agent may have already passed a background check, but get at least a few client references, and talk to them personally. Find out if the athletes think the agent is ethical, puts the client's interests first, and is knowledgeable about your sport and your league. If the answers don't satisfy you, consider another agent.

- Be sure you're clear on the terms of signing with an agent or agency. How long is the term of the contract? Does it have an opt-out clause? What recourse do you have if you are not satisfied with the agent's work? Does the contract allow you to take legal action against the agent or agency if that's warranted? Read the contract carefully.

- Warning signs that an agent may be a bad choice include excessive pressure to sign, negative stories from references, reprimands from a professional league, or trying to collect flat fees from you for representation instead of being paid a commission on what he's able to get for you in negotiations. A reputable agent won't ask you for a dime up front to represent you.

Solomon Wilcots, who played for the Cincinnati Bengals, Minnesota Vikings, and Pittsburgh Steelers as a free safety from 1987–1992 before becoming a successful broadcaster, explains:

> One of the biggest things was hiring my agent. I remember at the combine, I had all of these agents coming after me, and it was just a nuisance. They were coming at you so fast. And so furious. I just finally had to pick a lawyer in Boulder, Colorado.
>
> Today it's much more complicated because you're going to be discussing marketing deals. So as an agent, what else are you bringing to the table beyond just the ability to negotiate the contract? What are you going to do to help me enhance my ability to be drafted? These days they pay for guys to go to some off-site place to work out, and they pay for their nutrition. Being an agent is a whole different deal today.

YOUR BUSINESS MANAGER, YOUR COO

Writing on his website, retired thirteen-year NBA player Adonal Foyle has reinforced the fact that today's pro athlete is the CEO of a one-person branded enterprise. "Today's professional athletes are similar to many small businesses," he says. "The demands of the profession, the high amount of income, and numerous 'off the court' factors have some professional athletes choosing to hire a personal business manager. Often this is a close personal friend, family member, or representative from the agent's office."

An athlete's business manager is the assistant for a time when a twenty-five-year-old athlete might already have a massive social media presence, a video game contract, a record deal, a podcast, and six endorsement contracts. In other words, the days of just needing someone who can pick up your dry cleaning and keep track of your social calendar are over. You can use your iPhone and TaskRabbit for those things. Today, this job is all-encompassing. You need someone who can keep your business and financial affairs organized, secure, and timely. That's your business manager.

Your business manager could be a college teammate or family friend, but a preferable choice would be someone with a background in business, operations, or sports administration. This is the person who will manage all your day-to-day communications and transactions and let you know what's going on away from the playing field. Depending on what you need, an athlete's business manager might:

- Manage and pay your contractors—trainers, landscapers, security, and the like
- Negotiate contracts for appearances, speaking engagements, and the like
- Vet business opportunities and franchise offers
- Coordinate marketing and social media activity
- Handle financial traffic—bill-paying, tax payments, wire transfers, deposits in retirement accounts, rent collection, and so on
- Handle contracts for real estate transactions, big ticket purchases, property rentals
- Coordinate your live appearance calendar
- Work with your publicist to schedule interviews and television or radio appearances
- Make travel arrangements
- Collaborate with you on business and career strategies
- Act as a gatekeeper for anyone wanting to contact you
- Act as a "bad cop," saying no to people who want your time or money

In other words, your business manager will be an intimate player in virtually every phase of your life away from your sport. He or she should be someone smart, college-educated, business savvy, confident, and organized to a fault. You'll want a fearless negotiator with a memory like an elephant, a fiercely ethical person who isn't afraid to boss you around. That's hard to find, so take your time.

Finding Your Business Manager

Hiring your business manager is tricky because you're trying to find someone multiskilled who can be trusted in every nook and cranny of your financial and personal life, but there are no professional associations or set standards to help you find someone qualified and honest. So you're on your own. Here are some guidelines for conducting your search:

- Start with your fellow athletes and your agent. They are always your best resources for locating just about any service provider.

- Try to find someone with a business bachelor's degree and experience running a small business or nonprofit organization. Other areas of experience that are major plusses: marketing, sports management, public relations.

- Conduct a thorough background check. You know the old saying, "If it looks like a duck and quacks like a duck . . ." Reject anyone who has even a hint of bad behavior in their past.

- Get and check references.

- If you find a candidate, insist on a thirty-to-sixty-day probationary period. It's a test-drive. During this time give the prospective business manager nonconfidential, nonfinancial tasks to perform to assess his or her skills. You're looking to see if this person is thorough, organized, reliable, and a good communicator before you give him or her access to personal or financial information. During this period you're under no obligation to keep the candidate on.

- If you hire someone, insist that they sign a nondisclosure agreement (NDA). If they don't sign, they don't get the job.

- Your business manager should be comfortable working from home or a mobile office. Make sure they maintain online schedulers and other mobile tools so you can keep working when you're on the road and you don't incur the cost of an office.

- Finally, you're going to be giving your business manager some access to your financial accounts. After he or she starts work, have another party—your accountant, your financial advisor—confidentially keep an eye on account balances and financial activity, making sure nothing shady is going on. Trust but verify.

Unlike agents, business managers get paid a salary, usually in the range of $60,000 annually. While it might be tempting to fill the position with an independent contractor to avoid paying for things like benefits and payroll taxes, I'd advise you to make your business manager a full-time employee. The job is too important to hire someone who might be doing the same thing for four other athletes without you knowing.

YOUR FINANCIAL ADVISOR, YOUR CFO

Chris Dudley played for sixteen years in the NBA as a big man with the Cleveland Cavaliers, former New Jersey Nets, Portland Trail Blazers, New York Knicks, and Phoenix Suns. He also went to Yale, so when he retired in 2003, he earned his CERTIFIED FINANCIAL PLANNER™ professional designation and went into wealth management, making him uniquely qualified to comment on why athletes need financial advisors.

Chris said in our interview:

> I studied economics at Yale, and I think that if I hadn't played, I would've worked on Wall Street. A lot of times what you find is the more successful financial advisors are very good at sales, but they don't necessarily have the expertise. When I retired

from the NBA, I went and got my CFP® because I wanted to have the education behind me and I felt like with an economics degree and a CFP®, I'm as credentialed as anybody out there.

I think it's important that whoever you work with has had the education and is not just a salesperson. Wall Street wasn't built to educate the client; it was built to sell product. For me coming out, I wanted to get the credentials in insurance, estate planning, taxes, and investment. I mean, it's kind of a cost support. That doesn't make a CFP® an expert in all of them, but it makes you conversant in them. My approach was, I want to be sort of the quarterback and able to oversee everything right. That doesn't mean I want to be the person selling the insurance, but I want to be able to look at it to make sure the client's getting the right thing. Same with taxes or estate planning.

A financial advisor is your CFO and the third member of your Board of Directors—potentially the most important person you will hire. This professional is the boss of everything related to your finances, from accounting for every penny that comes in and goes out to tax minimization strategies and investment opportunities. On Investopedia.com, Amy Fontinelle writes, "Financial planning is a must for professional athletes, who are famous for burning through their six-, seven-, and even eight-figure salaries. Many pro athletes earn in a single year or a few years what the average worker may not see in a lifetime, but this can give a false sense of security."

Absolutely correct. As we've discussed, many professional athletes have an unusual combination of incredibly high earning potential, volatile peak earning periods that are often comparatively brief, high expenses, peer pressure to live costly lifestyles, and demands on their time that make it difficult to spare more than a glance at their account balances. That makes working with a qualified, certified financial advisor absolutely essential. As with a corporate CFO, your personal CFO ensures that you are positioned financially to sustain operations and grow for the future.

What Your CFO Does

I've identified four elements that make the financial planning needs of a professional athlete different from those of any other class of worker:

1. **Volatile earning peak.** This means that your time for earning high salaries or purses is relatively short and can end suddenly and without warning. Athletes with large guaranteed contracts can be protected from some of this volatility, but that's the minority. The mere mortals need smart, proactive planning to be a safety net in case their career ends abruptly.

2. **Income asymmetry.** Most nonathlete professionals start earning in their twenties or early thirties, then (assuming they're skilled and honest) their earnings climb until they peak, typically in their fifties or sixties. From there, the earnings glide path is often a slow, steady decline as they head toward retirement, though some individuals keep earning huge incomes through smart investments into their eighties and beyond.

    But pro athletes typically reach peak earnings in their late twenties to early thirties, and by age forty, that income stream is mostly gone, except maybe for some deferred money from a contract. (For example, MLB player Bobby Bonilla, as part of a contract buyout, is being paid $1.19 million per year, including a guaranteed 8 percent interest rate, from 2011 to 2036.) For the vast majority of athletes, there's no gentle glide path, just a Wile E. Coyote plunge with a puff of dust at the bottom. No other group earns 80 percent of their lifetime income with 50 percent of their lives still ahead of them.

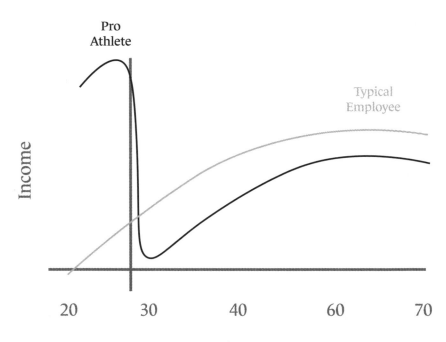

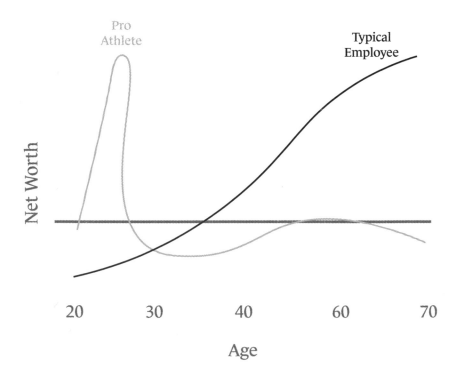

3. **One-way earnings path.** If a doctor, lawyer, or CEO retires and runs into financial difficulty, they can go back to work and probably earn close to what they were making when they left. Not you. Apart from losing a roster spot on a team, a pro athlete's skills and fitness quickly decline when playing days are done. You can't go back. That means you can only go forward, and *that* means finding new career paths and investments that can replicate much of the income you've left behind.

    The worst part is that all things being equal, if you as a veteran and a rookie are playing at the same skill level, the lower-cost athlete will get the job. You lose.

4. **"Soft target" syndrome.** One of the reasons fraudsters and unethical financial actors target jocks is that they're perceived as easy targets. According to the stereotypes, you're dumb, obsessed with materialistic possessions, and too busy to pay attention to your money. In a few cases, those stereotypes have proven to be true, and that's what attracts thieves. Your CFO must know how to keep your assets safe from all types of threats.

These four factors are why a personal CFO is mandatory. Your CFO is a trusted expert whom you put in charge of every aspect of your finances:

*   Developing a diversified investment portfolio and long-term asset management strategy

*   Advising you on business opportunities: venture capital, angel investing, franchises, launching your own brand—and their cash flow and tax implications—and structuring business entities such as LLCs and C corporations

*   Budgeting, bill-paying, and cash flow management

*   Tax planning and compliance, including advising you on ways to

minimize the "jock tax," tax-based options for where to establish your legal residence, proper tax deductions, and tax-advantaged contract structures

- Setting up and contributing to qualified retirement accounts and advising you on taking league pension distributions

- Managing debt—mortgages, credit cards, and so on

- Financial record-keeping

- Overseeing the rest of your financial team, such as your CPA and forensic accountant

Your financial advisor/CFO will work with you and the rest of your Board of Directors to create a comprehensive financial strategy that takes into account your short- and long-term goals, current lifestyle needs and expenses, career earnings potential in your sport, business interests, charitable interests, and much more.

Most importantly your CFO will get you on a real-world saving and investing program *right away*, since saving as much of your income as possible is the best way to avoid the spiral of debt and penury that befalls so many athletes after they stop playing, especially when their careers end involuntarily. Saving early is the key to sustainable wealth.

Mike Golic talks frankly about the abruptness with which a career can end and the importance of planning for it. He said in our interview:

> The best thing you can do is make all your connections while you're playing. Because when you're done, they don't care about you anymore. They love you while you're playing. So make connections while you're playing. Get your foot in different doors while you're playing. Get to know people while you're playing. That can lead to a smoother transition when you stop playing.

My career ended because all the teams didn't call anymore. I was basically retired. I didn't retire. The league retired me. Nobody wanted me anymore. That's how 90 percent of guys retire. We see the great stories of John Elway winning the Super Bowl and walking off into the sunset. That's fool's gold for the majority of pro athletes. You're ended because of an injury or because you're just not good enough anymore.

NFL tight end Rob Gronkowski, formerly of the New England Patriots but now catching passes from Tom Brady for the Tampa Bay Buccaneers, is a great example of preparing for that harsh reality. As of 2015, he said, he had not spent a dime of his signing bonus or his NFL salary, living on money from endorsements and appearances. "To this day, I still haven't touched one dime of my signing bonus or NFL contract money," he wrote in his book, *It's Good to Be Gronk.* "I live off my marketing money and haven't blown it on any big-money expensive cars, expensive jewelry, or tattoos and still wear my favorite pair of jeans from high school." That's living within your means!

Your CFO is also the quarterback of your financial team, directing and overseeing the activities of people like your CPA and tax expert. Finally, your CFO will be like Gandalf in *The Lord of the Rings*, shouting, "You cannot pass!" They are the educated, skeptical mind who reviews every plan to buy an expensive new car, boat, or condo and decides which of your buddies' businesses, if any, you'll invest in. Smart athletes hire a CFO they trust and then hand over the keys to their finances. Remember, money makes us all irrational. When you want that sweet new $160,000 G-Wagon or get a can't-miss stock tip from a teammate, it's your CFO's job to say, "That's not in line with your plan. Get the Escalade!" A great CFO will help you lead a smart, disciplined financial life while building a lifestyle you enjoy and saving for a bright future.

TIME-OUT

If you really want to dig deep into your CFO due diligence, request a copy of a financial advisor's Form ADV. That's paperwork filed with the SEC that details the advisor's compensation structure, training, education, business model, and any complaints or industry discipline.

WHY (AND HOW) TO HIRE A CFP®

Your CFO should be a CFP® professional. I don't just say that because I'm one. I say that because out of all the alphabet soup of designations you might encounter in the world of financial services, the CFP® is recognized as the standard of excellence in the industry. The CFP® is like your family physician—a general practitioner with some experience in everything who will also collaborate with specialists to get your finances as healthy as possible.

One reason the CFP® is the gold standard is that it's not an easy designation to earn. Before they can earn the certification, CFPs® must meet the requirements known as the "four Es"—experience, education, examination and ethics—and complete thousands of hours of training in seventy-two financial disciplines, including education planning, estate planning, tax planning, and retirement savings and income planning.

CFPs® must have at least a bachelor's degree and pass a rigorous six-hour exam that is the most difficult in the financial services industry. It's not an easy designation to earn. That's one reason that in 2018 the NFL required that all financial advisors it recommends to its players be either CFPs® or Chartered Financial Analysts (CFAs).

The CFP® matters for you because CFPs® are held to the highest ethical standards and all CFPs® are required to operate as *fiduciaries* for our clients. All financial advisors registered with the Securities and

Exchange Commission are required by law to act as fiduciaries, which means they must put your financial interests before their own and disclose any conflicts of interest. (Stockbrokers and insurance agents aren't required to be fiduciaries.) If your CFO is a CFP®, he or she can only do what it best for you or risk losing his or her license. Nonfiduciaries will keep their butts out of trouble as long as their advice isn't actively terrible, but they're not held to the highest standards. Working with a fiduciary protects you.

Apart from all the services they provide, a CFP® is also your connection to other important members of your financial team. I've been in the business for twenty years, and I can pick up the phone and in an hour have a roster of top-flight CPAs, tax attorneys, CFAs (another highly respected designation that focuses on investments, portfolio development and management, and asset allocation). I could even hook you up with forensic accountants and Certified Fraud Examiners to help if you have been the victim of a scam, but the sooner you start working with a financial team, the less likely you are to need those specialists.

Here's another way to look at the unique needs of athletes. The average person in the workforce might work from age twenty-two to sixty-five, retire, and live to eighty-five. So he only needs to fund his retirement for twenty years, less than one-fourth of his life. Two-thirds of his postcollege life funds the last third. But the professional athlete might play from age twenty-two to age thirty-two (if he's lucky) and then retire with more than fifty years of life ahead of him. Ten years of work have to fund a half century of retirement! This is why it's so vital for athletes to think and plan ahead, build multiple post-career income streams, and get good financial advice.

Athletes' need for sound guidance was brought home for me in a 2018 CNBC show called *Back in the Game*. In the show former MLB superstar Alex Rodriguez (who earned about $480 million during his MVP career) gave advice to and enforced discipline on retired athletes facing financial hard times. In the first episode, he counseled former NBA baller Joe Smith and calculated that while Smith had made about

$60 million in salary, he'd only taken home about $18 million. Still, not chump change. So where did it go?

As A-Rod found out, it went to overpaying for things like luxury cars, expensive mansions, and jewelry. By the time A-Rod came into their lives, Smith and his girlfriend had a monthly take-home income of just $2,000, a mind-blowing total of $133,000 in annual expenses, and $157,000 in debt. A-Rod helped them trim their expenses, live on a budget, and leverage Smith's NBA pedigree to boost their income.

But A-Rod, while a smart guy and a highly experienced investor, is not a licensed financial advisor. Imagine how much pain and financial loss Joe Smith could have avoided had he worked with a CFP® throughout his career to develop and execute a sound financial strategy instead of picking up the pieces after he was living week to week?

The answer is, all of it.

Choosing Your CFO

When choosing your CFO, the beauty of going with a CFP® is that the person is prevetted. He or she already has to abide by a fiduciary standard and complete a stringent set of licensing requirements. However, there are additional steps you should take to ensure that you're choosing the best person for your needs.

As always, talk to teammates or coaches and get referrals and references. Again, Mike Golic:

> Keep your mouth and your ears open, and learn from veterans. Learn how to go about your business from the financial side. Look at guys who are getting the kind of checks you're getting, and look at guys who have the same lifestyle. Talk to them: whom do they use? What happens, especially nowadays with all the money that's out there, is that a lot of companies will approach players.

> Even when I was playing, you would get letters from differ-
> ent groups that had this investment or wanted to handle your
> money. So you're going to get solicited to all the time. Trust
> your peers. Don't just hire the first person you see; see what
> they're doing for people. Talk to the player; talk to the player's
> wife. Do your research.

The recommendation of a teammate is not a guarantee, however. MLB star pitchers Jake Peavy and Roy Oswalt and NFL quarterback Mark Sanchez were defrauded out of a collective $30 million by a Registered Investment Advisor (RIA) named Ash Narayan, who had been warmly recommended to them by multiple teammates. When the SEC began investigating, it found that over a decade of working with these and other players and earning their trust, Narayan had funneled about $33 million into a company called The Ticket Reserve, in which he was a major shareholder. Given this, you can't stop at references. You need to keep digging.

Start with tools that let you investigate a prospective advisor's professional background. FINRA, the Financial Industry Regulatory Authority, which oversees all financial professionals and transactions in the US, operates a search engine called BrokerCheck (brokercheck. finra.org) that shows you an advisor's certifications, licensing, and more. I also recommend looking up financial services firms at sec.gov and learn more about their compensation, disciplinary action, and more.

You can also visit the CFP® search site, letsmakeaplan.org, or the Financial Planning Association website, plannersearch.org, to find good prospects. Your goal is to confirm that the advisor who's pitching you is licensed to act as a financial advisor and operates under the fiduciary standard. If either one proves not to be true, walk away. You should also ask lots of questions and have a financially knowledgeable party like your agent or CPA present while doing so. Some important questions to ask:

- **"How do you get paid?"** I can't emphasize too strongly how important it is to know this. Any reputable CFP® today is fee-based, meaning he or she gets paid either a flat fee, an hourly rate, or a set percentage per year of the assets he or she has under management. Most of the top CFPs® will get paid a percentage of the assets they manage for you. For example, your CFP® might earn 1 percent of the $1.6 million of your money he manages, or $16,000 annually. As your money grows, so does his income, which is a win-win. Do not work with advisors who are paid by commission for each financial transaction they complete. That simply encourages them to "churn" your account, issuing frequent unnecessary buy and sell orders to boost their commissions.

- **"What do you do for your athlete clients that you don't do for nonathletes?"** A CFP® who knows athletes and finance should be able to talk about the jock tax, endorsements, and issues like bonuses and deferred salary with ease.

- **"How do you communicate with your clients?"** You want someone who communicates regularly and in multiple ways—email, text, phone call, printed statement.

- **"What do you do to keep your clients' financial data secure?"** The advisor should have secure IT systems and security protocols in place, including having third-party identity protection services monitoring client financial and identity information.

- **"Will you sit down with me for quarterly account reviews and provide that information to my CPA?"** Reviews are vital because they're how you ensure that your CFP® is doing what he says he's doing. No reputable advisor should balk at providing statements to your CPA either. In fact, they should want to collaborate with other professionals to optimize your situation.

A few other steps can help keep you safe. First, exercise caution in giving power of attorney (POA) to your CFO. It's probably best to grant him or her *limited* POA. This allows your CFO to act on your behalf under limited circumstances that you specify. *General* POA, on the other hand, gives your CFO free rein over your financial accounts, and that's something I would not suggest granting. Discuss the specifics of limited POA with your CFO and your attorney. Also, be wary of misleading titles like "wealth manager" or "investment advisor." It seems like everyone is wearing one of those titles these days, but the problem is that those titles don't really mean anything. They don't tell you if the individual you're talking to has the professional certifications you need.

Finally, trust your gut. If you're getting the hard sell from a financial pro in the locker room or clubhouse but you don't like the answers to your questions, walk away. Live to fight another day. We have a saying in the business: "Return on investment is important, but return *of* investment is a lot more important." Unrealistic promises should raise red flags. Pay attention to them.

KNOW THE SCORE

If you are not yet working with a financial advisor or a financial team, you may have spending habits that work against you. Spending is most likely to become a problem when it's *invisible*—that's why Las Vegas casinos give you chips instead of letting you use cash and why credit card balances so often catch us by surprise. When we can't see how much is going out, it's harder to control what we spend. One tool you can use now to track your spending are *budgeting and financial tracker apps*. These are some of the best:

- You Need a Budget (youneedabudget.com)
- Intuit Mint (mint.com)
- Every Dollar (everydollar.com)

- Empower (empower.me)—this app is more about finding savings than budgeting, but that's helpful too.

THE SECOND TIER

The New York–based author and columnist Fran Lebowitz once said, "A dog who thinks he is man's best friend is a dog who obviously has never met a tax lawyer." I can't argue with that. Even after you've built your Board of Directors, you will need other members to be part of your team. No basketball team gets by with just its starting five, and no baseball team survives with just the pitcher and the infielders. You need others. These folks are specialists with specific but important roles.

They won't have the same access as your Board of Directors, and they won't have the same level of control over your finances. But they provide critical services. Your CFO or CMO might be able to connect you with reputable people so you don't need to spend your time searching for them. Let's take a quick look at who they are.

- **Attorney.** Unless you're one of the rare athletes who is a highly visible, highly paid star from the beginning of your career, you will probably not need an attorney on retainer early on. You can probably get the services you need via the lawyers in your sports agent's office, or you can have an individual attorney available on an as-needed basis to handle tasks like reviewing contracts, endorsement deals, and the like (which your agent could very well do for you).

    But as you become more successful, better-paid, and better-known, having an attorney on retainer becomes more necessary. Contract disputes, liability claims, defamation and nuisance lawsuits, paternity claims, and arrests for driving under the influence—these are all things that happen to athletes, and you'll want a good lawyer on hand if and when they do. In addition, having someone a text message away who's skilled in contract and business law could save you big if you're looking at an offer to represent a brand or invest in a start-up. You'll also want a lawyer to write your NDA, a must-have that we'll talk about later.

As with other skilled professionals, the best way to find a good attorney is to talk to your Board of Directors. Your CMO and CFO should have many highly regarded legal contacts.

- **Certified Public Accountant.** In the film *Schindler's List,* war profiteer Oskar Schindler memorably says, "My father was fond of saying you need three things in life—a good doctor, a forgiving priest, and a clever accountant." I couldn't agree more. The CPA is the gold standard among accountants, who are required to pass a rigorous licensing exam in order to practice. Your CPA will work with your business manager and CFO to ensure that your finances are organized, tracked, and legally bulletproof. This professional can assist you with:

  - » Paying taxes, especially given the complexity of the jock tax
  - » Setting up residency for tax purposes
  - » Paying agent commissions and union dues
  - » Charitable giving
  - » Record-keeping
  - » Determining favorable and legal tax deductions
  - » Collecting royalties
  - » Identifying potential fraud or identity theft

As always, your CFO or business manager probably has a CPA in mind for you, but if you want to conduct your own search, you can do it at aicpa.org.

- **Tax Advisor.** The waters get a bit murkier here. A tax advisor can be a CPA, an attorney with advanced training in tax law, or an enrolled agent, a tax practitioner authorized by the US Department of the Treasury. In any case, when it comes to taxes, you want a specialist who can then work with your CFP® and CPA to ensure not just proper tax preparation but also tax *planning*, the long-term strategy that keeps you on the right side of tax laws while ensuring that you don't pay a dime more than your legal obligation. (My preference is someone who is both a CPA and an attorney with an LLM, a postgraduate qualification also known as master of laws, with a specialty in taxation.)

Building the right team to handle taxes is critical for professional athletes. I have seen many, many athletes ruined by a failure to understand or properly address their tax issues. Athletes must pay taxes in every jurisdiction where they earn money, can legally reside almost anywhere, and have multiple potential income streams and levels of personal and professional expenses, and because tax laws are always changing, tax planning for professional athletes is incredibly complicated. Building a first-class team is your defense against penalties and interest that can be ruinous.

The issue of athletes and their taxes could be an entire book by itself, and we'll go into it more a little later. For now, rely on your CFO and CPA to find the right person or firm with the right set of skills and knowledge.

I can't emphasize this too strongly: having a tax advisor with experience handling taxes for pro athletes is a must. This not an area where you want someone who's learning on the job.

- **Publicist.** Again, you might not need a publicist early in your career because you're relatively unknown and focused on sticking with your team or in your sport and improving as a player. But later, if you become famous and want to turn your notoriety into business opportunities or a salable brand? You'll want someone to help manage your public image and reputation and to ward off threats from crazy fans and irresponsible journalists—as well as, occasionally, protecting you from yourself.

A publicist helps you play offense and defense with your public image. On offense, they will help you manage your social media accounts, land high-profile interviews, press stories, and personal appearances, and promote projects like charitable events or book signings. On defense, they'll help keep you from making damaging blunders on social media, counter negative and defamatory stories, and control the "spin." In this way, your publicist both *increases* your earning potential by making you more marketable and reduces financial losses by minimizing brand damage. If you hope to have a postretirement career in business, speaking, entertainment, or even politics, a great publicist can be your best friend.

Find publicists to interview by talking to teammates or your agent.

- **Security.** I know, I know. You can defend yourself. But personal security isn't about you squaring up with some drunk in a bar; it's about protecting you from threats you can't anticipate. For example:

  In 2002, Chicago Bulls star Jalen Rose and a passenger were stopped at a red light in the swank Brentwood neighborhood of Los Angeles when a car pulled up behind him. One guy got out, walked up to Rose's Bentley, and starting firing at the car. Rose took off, but his passenger was hit and ended up hospitalized. That's terrifying, and it's far from the only incident where a wealthy pro athlete has been targeted. It's the kind of thing personal security was meant to protect you from.

  Again, you probably won't need security early on. But if you become famous, the sad reality is there are people out there who will target you because they think you're rich or because they're mentally unstable. Yes, you can defend yourself, but the point of professional security is to *prevent* trouble and protect not only you but also the people you care about. A security agency's job is to make sure a physical altercation never happens in the first place by spotting threats and neutralizing them.

Some security companies will also protect your home, keep a close eye on personally identifying information (PII) like your Social Security number, and advise you on personal behaviors to avoid, such as not carrying wads of cash, wearing expensive jewelry, or making it rain at a club. Your agent and business manager should be able to advise you on your need for personal security, as should your teammates.

GOOD COP, BAD COP

I've made it clear so far that the idea of having a financial team is for the team to run every aspect of your financial and business life so you don't have to. Because you're not an expert, follow the model used by the world's most successful athletes, from LeBron James to Serena Williams: surround yourself with trusted smart people, be clear about what you want and don't want, and let them do their jobs.

Suppose you're considering an endorsement contract with a shoe company. Your agent would conduct the negotiations and report back to you, your CFO, and your business manager about the money, terms, length of the deal, product that was included in the deal, obligations for things like personal appearances, and so on. Your CFO would check with your tax advisor regarding the impact of the contract on your taxable income, possible deductions, and so on. He might also adjust your personal budget, retirement savings, and investment buckets to account for the additional income.

Meanwhile, your business manager would be talking with your agent about the effect of the deal on your travel schedule and other business commitments while your attorney did a double check of the contract and sent it back to the shoe company with any areas of concern red-lined. All this would come back to you through your agent and CFO, who would share the various pros and cons of this contract with you and advise you on the decision that best serves your interests. But the final decision will always be yours.

The main function of your team is to run your financial affairs, your brand, and your life like a highly efficient, profitable private company. But they have another important function: being the bad cop so you can still be the good cop. The members of your Board of Directors are your gatekeepers, the people who keep dumb stuff off your desk and say no to friends and teammates so you don't have to.

One of the most common reasons athletes wind up in financial difficulty is that they end up taking care of not only their family members but also their friends. Once you have money (or people *think* you have money), some will come to you with their hands out. They'll want jobs. They'll want you to float them a loan. They'll expect you to invest in their "unbelievable" business idea. Well, guess what? When you give your buddy $100,000 to open a bar or a tanning salon, the odds are it will go out of business in short order, and there goes your money.

That's what was happening with the NFL player I mentioned at the start of this chapter. He was listening to a business pitch that was obviously flimsy, and he shouldn't have been. When he finally got off the phone, I said, "Man, that is the kind of call you should not be taking. That's the kind of call you have your CFO take, and if it looks legit, he can bump it up to you. Otherwise, you don't waste your time." He loved the idea of having a layer of experts between him and the folks with their hands out, and that's one of the reasons he became my client.

Running all financial business through your Board of Directors means you don't have to say no to friends and family. You can stay the good guy. When one of the fellas comes to you needing money or pitching an investment, you can shrug and say, "Bro, I don't analyze that stuff. Get me a written proposal, and I'll put you in contact with my team, and they can look at it. That's how we've got things set up." That puts the call in the hands of people who are experts and who are objective, which is how it should be. It also eliminates emotion from the decision-making process. Anything that passes the smell test will get to you. The rest won't. By making your Board of Directors the "bad cop," you save face with your friends and family members and have your interests protected. You'll never have to be the bad guy.

CHECKS AND BALANCES

Your team is also here to protect you from your own poor decisions and from fraud within your team. Want to buy a house twice as big as what you need because you're competing with the guy whose locker is next to yours? Your COO will sit you down and remind you of your long-term plans and budget. Thinking of going on a spending spree with your Amex Platinum Card®? Your CFO can give you a quick primer on how much that debt is really going to cost you. Your team will save you from yourself occasionally.

Your Board of Directors will also save you from a bad call by another team member, because they oversee each other. Each person in your Board of Directors has equal power. The entire team should meet at least quarterly to discuss plans, outcomes, and so on. When decisions need to be made, majority rules. Don't let one person have too much control. That way, everything will be the result of fact-based, rational discussion, not impulse or emotion. That increases the likelihood of a positive outcome. This same arrangement also ensures mutual oversight. Make sure everyone is comfortable being monitored by someone else on the team. If someone gets their feelings hurt, make a change; there's too much at stake to worry about that.

Remember, your Board of Directors works for you. If you ever suspect that a member is acting in ways that are counter to your best interests, don't assume everything is fine. Ask questions. To limit the damage, have contingencies in place with your legal team that allow you to sever ties with a board member who's not acting on your behalf.

OVERTIME

Want to know a simple way to discourage the hucksters and well-meaning friends who come to you wanting an investment or loan? Ask them to put it in writing. Asking for a formal proposal is a completely reasonable request, but it will be too much trouble for 80 percent of people who were just expecting you to reach into your pocket and start peeling Benjamins off a wad as big as your fist. If someone does give you something in writing, you can always pass it along and let the bad cops do what you pay them for.

CHAPTER THREE

THINK LIKE AN ENTREPRENEUR

"As an athlete, your network is your net worth," says Chris "Macca" McCormack, the Australian triathlete and two-time Ironman World Championship winner regarded by many as the greatest in the history of the sport. In talking about his postretirement career helping foreign investors develop sports facilities in locales like Thailand and the Middle East, Macca says that building his network of contacts was everything. "We were trying to meet and build up a wider network in a new place like Asia, where (things were) moving so quickly." But Macca says that his background in accounting really set him up for success because as an individual competitor not attached to a team, he never lost sight of the need to build the business side of his career.

In Australia, rugby players make pretty much similar to what I was making at the top of my game. But it's not like Michael Jordan making two hundred million. When I started in my sport, there wasn't an expectation that at the end of this, I was going to be financially secure. So I didn't enter my sport with that mindset. I entered that sport with the mentality of "Okay, I'm going to achieve certain things," and then that became my profession.

I needed to be fiscally responsible in order to ensure that the outcome of the sport was not detrimental to my future. Regardless of having all these medals on the wall, if I don't have a wall to pin them on, then it's irrelevant, right? So I was relatively responsible quite young—and responsibility just comes with controlling spending. If I made a hundred grand, I lived as if I made a hundred grand. When I made four hundred grand, I still lived the same way. I didn't want for many things. I had a great wife, I had great friends, and I was always looking at my post-career. I was lucky to have a longer career, close to twenty years, and I spent the last ten of that making some substantial money, but that was relative.

McCormack says his annual earnings peaked at about $2 million, most of that from endorsements and sponsorships. But he was also responsible for all his expenses traveling to and from races, so he knew he needed to be businesslike in his approach to his future.

That's why I set up in Singapore, to be tax efficient. As an Australian passport holder, I could pay myself dividends and invest there. I was always interested in property because it made sense to me, so I bought a few properties. By the time I retired, I had enough to live for the rest of my life, but not to live the same lifestyle I'd been living. I probably would have had to continue working at some point to bring in money.

But I owned my home. I had a couple of investment properties. I had some money in the bank for a rainy day. Could I last the rest of my life without working? No, and I wouldn't want to do that. I love this lifestyle. I love the freedom that my children have. I love having opportunities for them. I enjoy what I do. I needed to maintain a certain revenue stream to do it. That was what I went after.

Indeed he did. Today McCormack runs Mana Group, a sports and entertainment agency, and helps develop and operate state-of-the-art sports and health resorts like Thanyapura in Phuket, Thailand.

It's relatively simple. You just treat [your post-career opportunities] with the same vigor and focus you brought to sport. It's just in another field, and it's actually easier. People are lazier outside of sport—they're in cruise mode. So if you understand that, you can navigate relatively easily and bring people with you once you understand what they want. It's not that difficult. Talking with people and convincing them that I'm worth investing in—that's what we did in triathlon, because triathlon is a niche sport, that is what I've sort of always done.

KNOW THE SCORE

You do *not* need to have a fifteen-year pro career and millions in earnings to turn pro sports into an entrepreneurial opportunity. Just having the words "professional athlete" in your bio can be enough. Take it from Malcolm Lemmons. He wasn't an NBA stud; he played pro basketball overseas for three years, but he was smart enough to realize that he needed a Plan B. He said in our interview:

I knew that I didn't want to play for ten-plus years. I didn't want to have such a long career that when I had to transition out, I didn't know how to do it. But it still ended up being a hard transition because I didn't know how to put a plan together. It wasn't until my second year playing overseas that I really started to think about what I would do when basketball wasn't in the picture. That's how I started to reflect on my experiences and some of the things that I went through as an athlete. How could I apply specific lessons and transition those skills to start something? I just started to write a lot and slowly but surely started to create a platform for myself.

That platform is Players Point Sports, an online platform and podcast dedicated to helping pro athletes successfully transition to a life after sports. He's also written two books, the latest being *Impact Beyond the Game: How Athletes Can Build Influence, Monetize Their Brand, and Create a Legacy.*

But Malcolm learned a really valuable lesson during those hard-scrabble years overseas: *hustle*. "The biggest thing that I took away was learning how to fend for myself and really market myself," he says. "In order to get a job, a lot of guys rely on their agents, but if you really want to stand out, you have to put yourself out there—email coaches and scouts and managers and all these different people. I had to learn how to promote myself and sell myself, not just rely on my agent. My career taught me how to survive."

TIME TO THINK LIKE AN ENTREPRENEUR

Chris McCormack knows his stuff. The moment you sign a contract with a team or commit to a professional athletic career, you become a brand and a business, and your ability to network and build relationships is the key to your success. So even after you hire your CMO, CFO, and COO and start building your AES, it's not enough. You have to start thinking like a business too.

If you think of yourself strictly as an athlete, you're shortchanging yourself. Why? Because presumably you want to have a life after sports, and you have a limited shelf life in the game. Unless your plan following the twenty-year span of your life that's been all about sports is to get a regular job, it's time to begin thinking of yourself as a business that will last long after you play your last game.

Keep in mind, there's nothing wrong with getting a regular job that has nothing to do with sports, but I can tell you that the athletes I've worked with generally don't want that. They've spent most of their lives in a pursuit that's given them a lot of pleasure: travel, competition against some of the best in the world, fitness, access to celebrities and political figures, and of course, the chance to earn some big money. Why would you turn your back on that when you could leverage your advantages to keep it going after the on-the-field action is over by developing and building on your business opportunities?

As a professional athlete, you have advantages in networking and relationship building that even someone coming out of the Harvard MBA program doesn't possess:

- The goodwill and prestige that come with being an active athlete. I've watched CEOs, venture investors, and real estate moguls fall all over themselves to shake hands with and work with pro athletes—not superstars, but average competitors. You have the power to charm and create excitement with your very presence, but the moment you retire, that's mostly gone.

- Press access. You know and can directly contact reporters, TV hosts, analysts, play-by-play guys, and more. That not only gives you a chance to generate publicity, but also gives you a path to a new career if that's something you're thinking about.

- You're famous (or semifamous). Okay, maybe you're not LeBron famous or Serena Williams famous, but in your sport, you're known. In your community, you're probably known. There's an air of celebrity associated with your name that's a huge edge for landing endorsements, getting people to take meetings, and generating publicity for a new company or product.

What I'm talking about is the professional athlete as an *entrepreneur*. An entrepreneur is someone who sees a need that's not being met and builds something to meet it—a company, a product, a network. Because of your short shelf life, and because of the inherent appeal that you have as a professional athlete, it's critical that you start thinking about how you can leverage your athletic career to boost your entrepreneurial career and to do that *as early as possible*. The earlier, the better.

Superstar Kevin Durant of the NBA's Brooklyn Nets is only in his early thirties and has lots of ball left in him, but he's all set for his post-career life. Along with his manager and business partner, Rich Kleiman he's launched Durant Co., a holding company with investments in Postmates, microlender Acorns, drone start-up Skydio, on-demand car company Yoshi, and many others.

It also pays to watch for opportunities and unmet needs within your sport and when they come, pounce on them. Former pro triathlete Nicole DeBoom did exactly that in 2004, when she won Ironman Wisconsin wearing a prototype running skirt of her own design. At the time there weren't any sports apparel lines designed for women's endurance sports, so Nicole retired and started Skirt Sports, a brand that's now racking up more than $10 million in annual sales.

Justin Forsett, who spent nine years in the NFL as a running back, did the same thing. Loved and respected around the league for his discipline, positive attitude, and community service, he noticed during his career that guys weren't always able to shower after workouts, leading to hygiene issues in the locker room. He and two UC Berkeley teammates invented ShowerPill, an antibacterial shower wipe for athletes, and the product was a smash hit. Today his company not only makes multiple hygiene products but has also been bringing PPE to underserved minority communities to help in the fight against COVID-19.

Athletes who enjoy financial security and success after their playing days don't just save and invest wisely. They are also opportunistic. They look for opportunities, just like entrepreneurs. They understand the relationship between risk and reward. This comes naturally for many athletes. After all, you're used to hard work and discipline. You're accustomed to setting goals and working toward them. You understand "systems thinking," where you are one cog in a bigger machine. And by virtue of making it as a pro, you have drive and grit far beyond the average business major.

TIME-OUT
Smart Postretirement Business and Career Moves

- **Media.** If you're comfortable on camera or in front of a mic and can find an experienced host or journalist as a mentor, you could build a long, fairly lucrative career as a broadcaster—and keep yourself visible, which is critical for your brand. Ex-jocks from Michael Strahan to MLB's Al Leiter to former skater Scott Hamilton have done this well.

- **Product line aimed at athletes in your sport.** Who knows better what the competitors in your sport need? This is the path some of the other athletes I've mentioned, Nicole DeBoom and Justin Forsett, have pursued. Creating and marketing products that solve problems you know all about is a smart path to entrepreneurship.

- **Rental properties.** Real estate often involves a big cash outlay, which can entail taking on lots of debt if you want to play big. That's why many athletes go smaller in the beginning, buying a handful of income properties and turning them into monthly rental cash flow. That's a terrific way to build wealth and learn about the inner workings of real estate—inspections, taxes, management, market ups and downs—while keeping your risk relatively low.

- **Franchises.** Buying into established restaurant franchises is incredibly popular among pro athletes for obvious reasons. These are established businesses with large customer bases, and if they're run well, they can be profitable for their franchisees right away. That's why players from MLB first baseman Adrián González (Jersey Mike's) to former NFL player Kris Brown (Dunkin' Donuts) have gone all-in on franchises. Buying into a highly successful franchise can be expensive—for example, you need to have at least $955,000 in nonborrowed personal wealth to become a McDonald's franchisee—but many successful athletes have that much cash, and the upside is incredible. If you don't have that kind of cash, try some of the lower-cost but highly regarded franchises in the *Entrepreneur* magazine Franchise 500, like Arby's, KFC, or Supercuts.

- **Spokesperson.** You've heard of the George Foreman Grill, right? Foreman started endorsing and selling the product long after he retired, and since he gets 40 percent of sales, he's made more money selling grills than he ever made in the boxing ring. If you've got a lot of charisma and a strong fan base, you could build wealth as a product spokesperson long after you're done playing.

- **Trainer.** Being an athlete is all about fitness, so some retired pros go into the fitness business. It makes sense. Devan Kline had a very brief career as a professional baseball player. He never even made it to the majors. But remember the "pro athlete mystique"? It's real, and he used it to found Burn Boot Camp, a women-only, indoor boot camp with more than two hundred locations (and more waiting to come online) and about $30 million in annual revenue.

- **Politics.** Not exactly a business, but politics can be a stepping stone to wealth and influence. Athletes, with their high visibility and name recognition, can be naturals to run for office. Examples include Kansas City Royals legend Frank White (County Executive for Jackson County, Minnesota), ex-wrestler Jesse Ventura (governor of Minnesota), NFL Hall of Famer Alan Page (associate justice on the Minnesota Supreme Court), and of course, former bodybuilder and actor Arnold Schwarzenegger (governor of California).

Thanks to the internet, you can get creative in earning extra income, if you've got a strong brand and fans still know and like you. One example is the web-based service Cameo.com, which lets fans pay for personal video greetings from celebrities. You can get a personal video message from Ice Cube for three hundred dollars, or from gravel-voiced comedian Gilbert Gottfried for one hundred fifty dollars. Small potatoes? Maybe. But Vince Papale thinks it's great, and he'll hook you up for fifty dollars. He told me on the phone:

I just got a couple of Cameo requests today, and it's been so uplifting. I'm getting emails and texts from people that I haven't heard from years. You know Pierre McGuire, the hockey guy? When I was playing, *Sports Illustrated* did a feature on me and they sent me around the country to do some speeches. I went to Hobart College, and I met Pierre McGuire. He was a hockey player at Hobart College. After the speech, he and his buddy— who was captain of the Dutch Olympic hockey team—let me play with them for a couple of periods.

> Pierre's one of my best friends now. And just today, through Pierre, I got two Cameo requests. One is for a girl who's concerned about her mother because she's a nurse and she's on the front line right now. She said, "Will you please send a message to her, just to let her know how much we care for her? We love her, and we're so proud of her."
>
> The other one was from a kid who's autistic, and his favorite movie is *Invincible*. I said, "Just give me his name and his phone number, and I'll send him a video." That's the beauty of this, that you can really have an impact on people.

Fifty bucks isn't much, but if you can make a few thousand dollars a year recording some videos for fans *and* grow your brand's goodwill at the same time, that's not an awful deal.

THE "THINK LIKE AN ENTREPRENEUR" PROCESS

All the successful entrepreneurs I've worked with share one specific character trait: They're competitive. They love to win. That gives you an edge because you're already wired that way. Still, a lot of athletes have no concept of the advantages they have or how to fully exploit them to build wealth. That's because being an entrepreneur is a matter of how you think, something Brett Flanigan knows well.

An Australian former men's basketball coach, Brett launched the Pro Athlete Entrepreneur Network (PAEN) to help retired and active athletes handle the shock of not being in the game anymore, build their professional networks, vet opportunities, and learn from each other. He says that one of the biggest deficits athletes bring to the entrepreneur's life is that for years they haven't had to build relationships. He says that the emotional toll of leaving the game hits hard and keeps them from exploring their options. He said in our interview:

No one's being taught to develop a relationship outside of school. That's criminal, because most of the professional athletes I talk to, they can't believe how quickly the phone stops ringing for them. They go from a very structured environment where they are around their teammates a lot, and then it stops. The very next week, in their teammates' eyes, that's the future they don't want to think about. It's like not wanting to be around somebody who's terminally ill.

We try and work with athletes' emotional and mental health. I haven't met an athlete yet who didn't need some kind of support. I'll meet a guy who says, "I'm all taken care of financially," but emotionally he's just a wreck. Then you'll have the other guy that emotionally is in a pretty good position, but financially he's just not ready.

PAEN brings athletes together to talk business, share opportunities and ideas, and learn from their peers, but the camaraderie is just as vital, Brett says. "We have regular monthly meetings where we bring the guys in in small groups," he says, "and they love the banter. They love to be around like-minded peers. They also like the challenge. That's been their whole life—they are competitive. We look to build in accountability. We talk about challenges, business advice, debrief everyone about their businesses and their goals. This sort of puts them back into a team environment, which is very satisfying for them."

Brett's organization had to go virtual because of COVID-19, but that didn't stop him. "The reason they joined the group is they want to be around each other and punch each other in the arm every now and then," he says. "That's really hard for us to replicate. But we're trying."

Network-building is one of the critical skills of the entrepreneur that athletes need to learn to build their post-career lives, but it's far from the only one. Let's look closely at the others:

1. Understand and safeguard your brand.
2. Find mentors.
3. Become an opportunity hawk.
4. Get educated.
5. Build your cash reserves.
6. Optimize your financial health.
7. Build your platform.
8. Respect the relationship between risk and reward.

1. Understand and Safeguard Your Brand

You have a brand that can be leveraged and has monetary value. That brand is your main product, and you need to make sure that it's not only clear but protected from damage. Some of that comes down to factors like personal behavior.

Vince Papale, who came out of obscurity at age thirty to make the Philadelphia Eagles as a walk-on back in 1976, becoming the oldest NFL rookie ever without college experience, has said:

> You've got to protect your brand. When I was coaching high school, the head coach from the high school was an FBI agent, and he had an intern who was actually monitoring the social media accounts of all of his players. He would warn them not to do something stupid, but every once in a while somebody would throw something out there and he would be gone, off the team. So you have to really be careful and understand whom and what you represent. If you want to take a stand for something, take a stand for the good things that are happening in the world. Stay away from politics; stay away from controversy. Do something positive. Go out and lend a helping hand for somebody.

What does your brand stand for? What personal qualities are you known for? What do people think of when they think of you? For example, early in his career, Michael Jordan was known for his high-flying dunks, and that led to the creation of the Air Jordan brand by Nike, the most popular athletic shoe line in history. Shaquille O'Neal, on the other hand, was well-known for his grin and playful, boyish attitude toward life and basketball, and that turned into a career in movies and TV shows. *Know what you stand for.*

It's just as important to fully develop your brand. Think about the iPhone. It's an incredible product, right? Your skill set as an athlete and your persona on and off the field are your product—your version of the iPhone. But as cool as the iPhone was when it first came out, it was nothing without Apple behind it. Apple did the research and development. Apple did the sales and marketing. Apple made sure there was quality control and all the employees were doing what they were supposed to be doing. That's why people lined up to get the early iPhone. Your goal is to be Apple, to build an enterprise around your product.

Developing your brand is about carefully curating what products, companies, causes, and people you will be associated with in the minds of consumers. It's also about being hyperaware of what's being said about you in the press and on social media. I'll talk about the press and social media later on, so let's stay on the first topic. No one can legally attach your name or likeness to anything without your permission, so it's up to you and your team to become ruthless guardians of your image. Once you decide what you want to stand for and how you want to be known, only associate with products or companies that reflect those same qualities.

A brand is a promise, and when you make that promise to the public, it's vital that you keep it. Let's say that you promote yourself as being all about family values. But then a chain of strip clubs asks you to be its spokesman and you say yes. What are your fans likely to conclude? That you're a hypocrite, and nobody likes a hypocrite. Your actions and company must be consistent with your brand promise.

If you build a popular, consistent brand with strong support in social media and the press, you can leverage it in a broad array of ways:

- **Lending your name to products as an endorser.** As you know, athlete endorsements of products and the use of athlete names and likenesses to lend an air of celebrity to products is a huge industry. For example, through mid-2019, MLB superstar Bryce Harper had earned about $45 million through endorsements that included Under Armour, barbershop chain Blind Barber, Gatorade, and MusclePharm, among others.

- **Being a social media influencer.** In 2017 soccer superstar Christiano Ronaldo signed a $1 billion lifetime endorsement deal with Nike, largely due to his huge social media footprint, which at the time reached about 260 million people. But you don't have to have that kind of monster audience to earn an income thanks to your social media profile. So called *microinfluencers* and *nanoinfluencers*—people who "only" reach a few million or a few hundred thousand highly desirable consumers—can still earn endorsement or paid promotional income from brands for social media activity that moves the sales needle, such as tweeting a positive review of a sports drink or piece of equipment.

- **Radio or TV hosting.** This is another common path for retired athletes to stay close to the game they love, associate with some of the teammates and opponents they miss, stay in the public eye, and sometimes, make some pretty good money. For instance, former NFL defensive lineman Mike Golic (whom we've heard from in these pages) earned $5 million as the cohost of ESPN's *Golic and Wingo* show. Not every ex-jock will make that much, but it's not out of the question. Companies like the Marc'd Academy (run by TV reporter and anchor Marc Watts) and the NBA's Sportscaster U program (which has taught hoops luminaries ranging from Charles Barkley to Richard Hamilton) train interested athletes in the skills of a broadcaster and often help them find jobs and manage their careers.

- **Author and speaker.** From David "Big Papi" Ortiz to the aforementioned Chris "Macca" McCormack to *Alone on the Wall* by near-mythical pro rock climber Alex Honnold, athletes have been turning their glamour and audiences into book deals for decades. Often a book deal leads to engagements as a motivational speaker, and that's where athletes with charisma and skill as speakers can really earn a nice income. Well-known stars working with top speaker bureaus like Washington DC's Keppler Speakers Bureau can earn tens of thousands of dollars for a keynote speech and speak dozens of times a year.

- **Sports agent.** Finally, what better way to leverage your experience and smarts than to represent athletes from your sport in contract negotiations? A great place to start in this career is by going back to school to earn a degree in sports management—degrees in law and business are also desirable—but that's not essential. Probably the best way to learn about becoming an agent is to pick the brains of some of the agents you've worked with and see if you have what it takes.

2. **Find Mentors**

   One of the best ways to learn about being a sports agent, a broadcaster, a speaker, or just about anything else is to find experienced mentors who will share what they know and introduce you to other key players in the field. That's true in any profession but especially in the tight-knit world of pro sports, where everybody knows everybody. As you prepare for your entrepreneurial future, make a conscious effort to seek out mentors in the fields you're interested in, whether they're veteran broadcasters or experienced real estate developers who can show you the ropes of investing in new properties. Finding mentors is an important part of building your network.

3. **Become an Opportunity Hawk**

   It's critical to understand how you can monetize your notoriety and success. Remember that as a professional athlete, people will invest their time and money just to be around you. Remember Vince Papale, whom we heard from earlier? He played in the NFL for just three years on special teams, but his story was so inspiring that it ended up being made into a 2006 movie, *Invincible*. Papale has parlayed that into two books and a busy speaking career. That's the power of being an athlete. You're a hero.

Start honing your ability to spot opportunities to monetize your brand and your name. There are quite a few:

- **Investment opportunities.** Doug Brien was drafted out of UC Berkeley in 1994 as a placekicker by the San Francisco 49ers and enjoyed a solid eleven-year career in the NFL. After he went back to school while in the league and learned about real estate, retirement led him into the world of business and start-ups. Then in 2008, when the real estate market and the entire economy were collapsing, Doug and a friend, Colin Wiel, noticed something that no one else seemed to catch: while the price of homes was plummeting in California's San Francisco Bay Area (like everywhere else), rents were staying stable. That meant an investor could buy single-family homes at low prices but still generate healthy cash flow in rents. No one else was moving on this opportunity, so Doug and Colin did, eventually building their company, Waypoint, which years later was part of several multibillion-dollar mergers.

  Become obsessed with business and financial news. *Forbes*. *CNBC*. *Fox Business*. The *Term Sheet* e-newsletter. *Kiplinger's*. Network with people in real estate, venture capital, franchising, and the financial markets. That's how you get wind of deals like undervalued assets, companies going on the block, and great real estate deals. Hone your instincts and learn to always be scanning the horizon for new investments—like a hawk.

  It also wouldn't hurt to become friends with financial and business mavens and even have your own weekly roundtable over a drink to talk about opportunities.

- **Starting your own business.** You've read about many athletes who've created products and started their own companies. It's a smart move because you're already known. The biggest challenge for any start-up business is letting people know you exist, but in your hometown, you're probably already newsworthy. That gives you a huge edge. For instance, Brent Hayden is a Canadian swimmer, a 2012 Olympic bronze medalist, and a world champion. Now, that's not a resume that suggests *huge* business prospects, but Brett knew how to use his position in the world. He started an athletic wear company, Astra Athletica, with a brand tied to the subject matter of his motivational speeches—namely, overcoming the limitations of body, mind, and soul to win.

- **Allying with a brand that complements you.** If there's one former athlete who gets the concept of leveraging what you have to work with, it might be Dennis Franks. An offensive lineman for the Philadelphia Eagles and Detroit Lions from 1976–1979, he didn't make a fortune in his pro career. However, he really made his career pay by using it as a stepping stone to go from the labor-intensive work of running franchises to network marketing giant Market America.

    Frank said in our interview:

> My experience building wealth came when I started learning about residual income. When I understood that I no longer had to exchange my time for money, it changed everything in my life. I never did anything for immediate pay; I did everything for the residuals. Being in a traditional business was very hard—having employees and all that other stuff. [So I went] back into network marketing, and I drew upon the residual income to help continue to pay for the franchise operations.
>
> Ultimately, I met J. R. Ridinger, the founder of Market America, back in May of 1992. For twenty-eight years now, I

have been involved with that company. I evolved to become their executive vice president in 1993. I was gifted a percentage of the company, which at the time was a start-up, so not worth a whole lot, but today it's worth well over a billion dollars, and it's turned into something great. We've created an organization of some two hundred thousand independent contractors serving six million customers, and we now have offices in eight countries. We went public for a period of about eight years, and then we bought the stock back and became a privately-owned company today.

I asked Franks what made him successful in a venture that was so far outside his experience. "Number one, respect," he said. "Number two, team building, being a professional networker. Number three, realizing that you have to find a business that can reinforce what you have."

Amen. If you're spectacular at inspiring people, partner with a coaching company. If you're brilliant at selling, hook up with a firm like Market America. If you're all sports, all the time, partner with a company that designs stadiums or sports video games. If you love kids, become the face of a nonprofit that helps children. Find partners that lift you up.

- **Partner with other players to buy a team.** You might not be Derek Jeter or Magic Johnson, but you also don't have to buy the Los Angeles Dodgers or Miami Marlins. There are teams at all levels—minor league baseball, the NBA's G League, the WNBA, pro lacrosse, American Arena League football, the American Hockey League, and many others. Putting together a team of athletes, management pros, and financial people to buy a team is a great way to invest, stay connected to sports, and learn about sports management.

- **Being a success coach or motivational speaker.** I've mentioned professional speaking in talking about ex-athletes like Vince Papale, but there's also a market for former players as success coaches, primarily in the business world. You've spent a lifetime being all about commitment, discipline, perseverance, hard work, and being part of a team—all qualities that corporations would kill to have their people be better at. Why not turn those qualities and your experience into a career that you control?

Todd Stottlemyre spent fifteen years as major league pitcher, winning 138 games. But today, after some time working on Wall Street, he's a high performance business coach, speaking to companies and business audiences about failure, fear, and going after their dreams.

- **Becoming a coach or manager.** This is the obvious choice, right? Once your active playing days end, just stay in the game as a coach or manager. That can be a terrific option for some players, but not all. Not everyone can teach, and teams tend to hire players as coaches who were affable and coachable themselves—players who demonstrated good character, were willing to learn, were hard workers, and so on.

  But if that's you, even if you were a mediocre pro athlete, who knows? You might become a star as a head coach or manager. After all, MLB manager Joe Maddon, former LA Lakers head coach Pat Riley, NHL coach Ken Hitchcock, and legendary Pittsburgh Steelers head coach Chuck Noll were not good professional players. But once they transitioned to coaching, their natural gifts came out, and they became legends.

BE CAREFUL WITH PRIVATE BUSINESSES

Lastly, know the types of "opportunities" to avoid, especially bars and restaurants. I can't tell you how many athletes I've talked to whose sad stories revolved around sinking a few million into a high-concept bar or restaurant idea, only to watch the business sink right along with their investment. Running a bar sounds like a lot of fun, but the food and entertainment biz is insanely competitive and runs on very thin margins—and, according to GetOrderly.com, restaurants in the US have a *60 percent* failure rate in their first year. You can find better places to put your money.

Do not invest more than 20 percent of your net worth in privately-owned businesses. Also, don't put that 20 percent into just one business. Diversify. Don't put all your eggs into one basket. Spread the risk around.

Most importantly start *now*. Start finding and pursuing opportunities today, while you're still active. That's when you have the cachet. That's when you're magic. That's when you can fill a room. Begin building for the future and finding those golden opportunities now, before retirement forces you to.

4. Get Educated

This doesn't necessarily mean going back to school, although I highly recommend it if you're interested in being a player in finance or technology. (Getting your MBA is *always* a good idea.) But getting an education can also mean going where the action is and learning from the experts in the real world. "Kevin Durant, the reason he went to California was to learn about the tech industry so he could invest," says Brett Flanigan. "LeBron goes down to Los Angeles. Did he go because he wanted to learn about the Lakers? No, he wanted to learn about Hollywood."

There are also private companies that help athletes learn about entrepreneurship. SeventySix Capital's Athlete Venture Group allows players to invest, learn, and work directly with top sports tech start-ups and entrepreneurs. Their athletes include Pro Bowler Brian Westbrook and NBA Hall of Famer Ralph Sampson. I also recommend trying my Financial Literacy for Athletes video program, which gives you more than eight hours of easy-to-understand financial education for just $99. Find it at WealthLit101.com.

These days, between mentors, private firms, educational programs in business, real estate and other specialties, traditional universities, online universities, and online learning companies like Khan Academy, there is no excuse for any athlete not to spend some time in the offseason becoming familiar with computer programming, apparel design, or the ins and outs of options contracts. If you really enjoy a subject, dig deeper—if you're fascinated by Wall Street, consider taking the required courses and testing for your Series Seven securities dealer license. Whatever you're interested in, there are resources to help you learn.

Education can also mean career training, as Solomon Wilcots explains:

The league built itself on the backs of some of these guys who are now broke; it's embarrassing for the league. So there was a concerted effort between former players, the league, and the union, all coming together. I worked for years as part of our broadcast boot camp, teaching players the skills to go into broadcasting. It was a joint venture between NFL films and the union and the league. Players had to write letters that showed their academic acumen to be able to participate and thrive in a program like that. Now you have the deal at the Wharton Business School, Harvard, and Northwestern. Now players can get continuing education, and even get their MBAs. Players have always been smart, despite this thing about athletes being dumb.

5. Build Your Cash Reserves

Early on you should save a healthy percentage of your take-home income as a cushion in case of financial emergency. I'll go more into this later, but here's the basic formula. Figure out how much money you need to live on for a full year, including rent or mortgage payments, car payments, food, utilities, phone bill, travel, and gas. Save 75 percent of your take-home pay in a bank account until you reach that amount. Then forget about the account. That's your emergency money, the cash you can turn to if you get injured, have a big medical bill, or need to hire an expensive lawyer.

Suppose you play pro tennis with solid success. You aren't Serena Williams, but you haven't embarrassed yourself. With tournament prizes and money from endorsements and personal appearances, you earn an average of $750,000 per year and take home $400,000 after taxes—about $33,000 a month. You're single and live fairly simply, so twelve months of living expenses for you equals $150,000. You save 75 percent of that $33,000 every month—about $24,750—until you get to $150,000, which takes you about six months. That's your emergency safety net, money that's safe and liquid, so you can access it easily if you need it.

Once you have a year's expenses saved, stop. Don't tie up any more of your income in low-interest accounts, because you want that money working for you in the market, earning higher returns.

6. **Optimize Your Financial Health**
   In other words, get your shit together. The last thing you want when you're done playing and exploring that franchise opportunity or income property is to get turned down for a loan because your credit rating is lower than a snake's belly. Ideally, your financial team should be paying attention to this and making sure things like credit card bills are always paid on time. But in case you haven't taken my advice and built your inner circle of financial and business wizards, here's what to do:

- Check your credit scores at the three credit rating agencies: Experian, Equifax, and TransUnion. This will usually cost you about forty dollars and will not ding your credit.

- If your scores are low—below 700 is too low—then pull your credit report, which lists all your credit-related transactions. You're entitled to a free copy of your credit reports once a year from each credit bureau. Get it by visiting www.annualcreditreport.com. When you get your reports, scrutinize them with the help of your CPA. You're looking for errors, fraud, transactions you don't recognize. Anything that looks wrong, dispute it with the credit agency.

- Make sure you pay your bills on time. Have the payments automatically deducted from your checking account so they're never delinquent.

- Pay down your debts as much as possible. Using too much of your available credit lowers your score, and lenders won't lend to you if you're overextended.

- Don't go near those "don't let the credit card companies trick you" debt settlement outfits. They're scams, and their "services" can crap all over your credit score.

- When you have your financial life in order and humming along like a Swiss watch, lenders will treat you with more respect. They'll offer you better loan terms. Business partners will see you as an asset, and would-be partners will be more likely to say yes to an opportunity to work together. Most importantly you won't have financial booby traps hiding in the dark, waiting to go off and wreck what you're trying to build.

7. **Build Your Platform**

Finally, thinking like an entrepreneur means making sure your number-one asset, your notoriety as a supercool former athlete, stays strong. That means building up your visibility platform by continuing to get coverage in the press and by growing your audience on Twitter, Instagram, Facebook, TikTok, and YouTube.

When it comes to the press, it's a no-brainer. Hire a publicist. They're not cheap, but a good press rep will ensure that you're getting covered in the broadcast, print, and online media with regularity. As for social media, we've already talked about the power it has, the potential for huge income it offers if you build a huge audience and have a lot of influence. I know, you're not a Kardashian, but you have a reach, and you can still engage fans. Imagine what a few million Instagram followers would do for your start-up business or your new product on sale now at Target! If you're not sure how to build your social media audience, Google "social media agency for athletes" and you'll find a lot of great companies to help you.

8. Respect the Relationship Between Risk and Reward

You understand that reward requires risk. Every time you take the field, run onto the court, or step into the ring as a professional athlete, you accept the risk of a career-ending injury and even damage to your long-term health. In return for taking that risk, you have the potential to reap incredible financial rewards. Finance works the same way.

In investing, low levels of uncertainty are associated with low potential returns. Your money might be very safe in a savings account, but you'll only earn about a half percent in interest (if you're lucky). High levels of uncertainty come with high potential returns. That's why some hedge funds, which tend to be more aggressive and riskier than instruments like mutual or index funds, sometimes give investors huge returns.

As you build your financial future, one of your responsibilities is to identify the risk tolerance you're comfortable with. Talk with your Board of Directors, especially your CFO, about the risk levels of different categories of investments, from stocks to real estate to venture capital. Then work as a team with your Board of Directors to identify investments that balance your risk tolerance with your goals.

Want a comfortable life and a nice retirement with little drama? A more moderate risk profile is for you. But if you aspire to build an empire in real estate, franchises, or what have you, you will have to accept greater levels of risk for the potential of massive returns. Bottom line, to grow your money and build the lifestyle you want, you will have to get comfortable with some level of risk. It comes with the territory.

TIME-OUT

If there's anyone who's done entrepreneurship right, it's former Olympic gymnast Shannon Miller. A seven-time Olympic medalist and one of the most decorated athletes in US history, she retired from her sport at nineteen. *Imagine that.* But she didn't mess around: she earned her undergraduate degrees in marketing and entrepreneurship from the University of Houston and her law degree from Boston College and then launched her company, Shannon Miller Lifestyle: Health and Fitness for Women, in July 2010. Diagnosed with ovarian cancer in 2011, she didn't miss a beat, going public with her treatment (and hair loss), writing a book, and speaking about women's health even as she was getting chemotherapy. Today, she's cancer-free and a product spokesperson, a motivational speaker, has her own line of dietary supplements, and runs a foundation dedicated to fighting childhood obesity. In other words, she combines not one but *two* inspiring stories, a personal mission, education, and business savvy. Any athlete could do a lot worse for a business role model.

RUN YOUR LIFE LIKE A BUSINESS

Writing in *Inc.* magazine, Brian Scudamore, founder and CEO of O2E Brands, stated, "I run my life the same way I run my company: with streamlined systems and processes to guarantee success."

Tattoo that on your bicep, please. Because that's what I'm talking about here. If you want to build massive wealth after your career and establish multiple streams of income that don't depend on you playing sports, you have to start—right now—running your life like a business.

That begins with paying close attention to every part of your personal and professional life, from your friends to your spending habits, and assessing each one objectively. Each is either a potential asset for your prosperous future or it's a liability. Time to put rules, systems, and people in place to get each under control—to take advantage of the assets and minimize the liabilities, so to speak. I'll go into that in depth in the following chapters.

The other thing you'll have to do to run your life like a business is to think of yourself as what you are: *your product*. If you're still active, then that product is your athletic prowess and your public popularity, which you'll sell to brands for lots of endorsement dollars. After your career ends, you're selling other things: your pro athlete mythology, the prestige of your championships, your storytelling, your smile, your fitness, your voice, your image, your community presence, or your power to bring people out for a cause. You are your product. It's the job of You, Inc. to ensure that the product remains of the highest quality and that you're getting the most possible value for it.

As Scudamore said, running a successful business means having *systems* in place. Profitable businesses don't make shit up as they go; they don't randomly spend capital or trust people they haven't vetted. Why should you? You are a business, and this is your mission statement:

Fully leverage every dollar's worth of economic value from my unique standing as a professional athlete, in keeping with my athletic talents and personal ethics.

In other words, you want to get as much as possible out of the high pay, commercial opportunities, unique standing in the community, and special prestige that comes with being a pro athlete, and you want to do it in a way that lets you keep your integrity. Right? Good. The first thing to do is something we've already talked about a lot: *build your team*.

The next thing you need is a *business plan*. No business just says, "Hey, let's maybe try to do $5 million in sales this year, and hire—I don't know—twenty people; what do you guys think?" Any good company has a plan for growth, hiring, marketing, raising capital, and so on. What's your business plan? It should take you at least five years into the future and account for:

- Whether you'll be active or retired
- An annual income goal
- Income sources—salary, endorsements, rental income, royalties, and so on
- The investments in your investment portfolio
- A savings target
- Projects you would like to undertake
- People you'd like to be working with
- Possible threats to your prosperity and how you can deal with them
- Possible opportunities to pursue
- Personal development goals (getting your degree, etc.)

RUN A TIGHT SHIP

If you're a business, then *your home life should be run like a business*, not like a frat house. No more buddies hanging out and sleeping on your couch every night. No more giving your cousin $20,000 to invest in his "sick" business idea. No more lending your friends money all the time with no accountability. No more unnecessary risks that could create liability or damage your brand. You don't have to be boring, but take this seriously. You only get one shot.

Next, *start looking strategically at the opportunities* around you right now. What are your areas of interest? Do you have the inside track on investing in a promising business? Is the real estate market in your city undervalued? Develop an entrepreneur's eye; think in terms of cash flow, appreciation, market share, and annualized returns. If you're not sure what those things are, that's fine—partner with someone who is. There's probably a lot of untapped opportunity around you that you're not even aware of. Remember, an entrepreneur is someone who creates something from nothing—who takes a calculated risk and turns it into a reward.

Also, figure out ways to *connect with the people who will be sources of future opportunities*. LinkedIn is a terrific resource, but there are also virtual and live networking groups like PAEN, which I mentioned earlier. In your city, there are almost certainly business and entrepreneur networking organizations, including some run by your chamber of commerce. Take advantage of them. Trust me, as a pro athlete, you'll be the star of the show.

Screen every offer and opportunity. In public, welcome every overture and idea. Smile and be grateful and obliging. In private, sitting around the table with your team, be skeptical as hell. Don't believe the hype. Run the numbers. Check everyone's background. Get every relevant expert's opinion on every opportunity—what it will mean for your taxes, how it could affect your child support, what the risks are, and so on. Be cautious. If the opportunity is legit, it will still be there in a week, after you've done your due diligence. Anyone who insists that you have to "invest now or you'll lose your chance" is either trying to cheat you or has seen one too many movies. That's the used car salesman tactic: "The price goes up on Monday!" It's the oldest trick in the book. Don't fall for it.

KEEP YOUR FINANCIAL LIFE EFFICIENT

Being a business means letting your accountants keep the books. Make sure bills are paid, accounts are balanced, insurance is sufficient, and your money has been allocated to the proper accounts. In other words, all you should have to worry about is making sure your credit cards are in your wallet and that you have enough cash to cover the night's expenses.

Establish an office away from your home where you can conduct business and only business. It's fine if it's a suite at a WeWork location; that's actually smarter than leasing space. But keep home life and business life separate. That helps maintain security for business accounts, keeps at-home emotion from affecting business decisions, and ensures that when you're home, you can *be* home with your family, no business allowed.

Legally protect your asset—yourself. If you've established designs, logos, or other intellectual property around your brand, talk to a trademark and patent attorney about legal protection. If you find that someone has illegally used your name or likeness or has defamed you in print or online, lawyer up and make them stop. Be sure to follow personal security protocols like we talked about before—changing passwords and so on.

(Be smart about the whole IP protection thing, though. LeBron James's company, LBJ Trademarks, actually attempted to trademark the term "Taco Tuesday." The US Trademark and Patent Office sent that shot back in LeBron's mug like they were Dikembe Mutombo, stating that the term is "a commonplace term, message, or expression widely used by a variety of sources that merely conveys an ordinary, familiar, well-recognized concept or sentiment message." As the late Chick Hearn would have said, that's *gotta* hurt.)

FINAL MEASURES

I've talked about the importance of hiring a publicity firm to manage your image, but it's also vital to have a crisis plan in place, just as every large company does. What will you and your Board of Directors do if a media outlet runs a false story about you, someone accuses you of sexual harassment, or one of your companies is sued? In a crisis, emotions can run high and you can forget about important steps, but if you have a written plan in place, everyone knows what has to happen when and knows his or her role.

If you want to get involved in charitable giving, look at the issues and causes you care about most, and either work with existing charitable organizations or foundations or create your own. The sports world is filled with outstanding nonprofits founded by athletes who want to give something back to the community. A well-run charitable organization is a win-win for you: it improves your image in the community, gives you tax benefits, and builds goodwill for your brand.

Finally, update your AES from time to time, adding new people to the team as your situation changes. If you're investing in businesses, perhaps an investment banker should be at the table. If you're dabbling in commercial real estate, maybe a real estate broker needs to be on the team. If your public image is growing more prominent, invite your publicist to meetings. Businesses adapt and change with the times. So should you.

Now, let's move on and talk about specific areas of your lifestyle and finances where small changes can yield big benefits.

OVERTIME

Some outstanding resources for learning about entrepreneurship and business:

- edX.org
- KhanAcademy.org
- MIT Open Courseware Entrepreneurship Courses (https://ocw.mit.edu/courses/entrepreneurship)
- OpenCulture Free Business Courses (http://www.openculture.com/business_free_courses)
- Alison.com (https://alison.com/courses/business)

- Sacramento Entrepreneurship Academy (https://www.sea-link.org/)
- AtLETyC (http://atletycmooc.eu/)
- Athlete Network (https://www.athletenetwork.com/)
- Entrepreneur On Fire podcast (https://www.eofire.com/podcast/)
- University entrepreneurship academies:
  - » Bowie State
    bowiestate.edu/academics/special-programs/entrepreneurship-academy/
  - » The Wharton School, The University of Pennsylvania
    https://online.wharton.upenn.edu/entrepreneurship/
  - » Illinois Institute of Technology
    web.iit.edu/entrepreneurship-academy
  - » Georgetown
    summer.georgetown.edu/programs/SHS10/entrepreneurship-academy

CHAPTER FOUR

YOU'RE NOT A BANK

By the time he was twenty years old, Antoine Walker had won an NCAA basketball championship with the University of Kentucky and been selected in the first round of the NBA draft by the Boston Celtics. During a thirteen-year career in the league, he was named to three All-Star teams, won an NBA ring with the Miami Heat, and earned an estimated $108 million in salary. Yet Walker has become a cautionary tale, an example of how a careless or unwary athlete can blow through any pile of money.

It wasn't just that Walker spent like a sailor on leave (reportedly never wearing a designer suit more than once) and dropped huge bankrolls at Las Vegas casinos. It was also that he was handing out cash to family and friends like the stuff grew on trees. At one point, he claimed that he had given money to about *seventy* friends and members of his family over his career. "I gave them whatever they wanted and spoiled them. You can't do that," Walker said to CNN Business. "I ended up being an open ATM throughout my career."

In 2010 Walker filed for chapter 7 bankruptcy after his real estate company failed during the financial crisis, and the following year he was charged with writing more than $1 million in bad checks to cover his gambling debts. He's said that the real estate crash was the primary cause of his financial misery, but let's be honest, being a piggy bank to dozens of people certainly didn't help.

Today Walker works (along with several other retired pro athletes) as a consultant with EdYouCore, a firm that educates people in sports and entertainment to make better financial, business, and lifestyle decisions.

WITH FRIENDS LIKE THESE, WHO NEEDS CREDITORS?

When you finally make it as a professional athlete, nobody is happier for you than your family members and longtime friends. They've been there from the beginning, watching as you played in the street in your neighborhood, starred in high school and maybe in college, worked out until you puked, and paid the price in the gym and endless practices to get good enough to be drafted or compete alongside the best in the world. Most of them want nothing more than to cheer you on and celebrate when you win, and some of them can become real assets during your career. This was illustrated in a piece written by Luke Petkac for Bleacher Report:

> A picture has been painted of NBA stars' friends and family mostly being bottom-feeding leeches who are just there for the money. That can be true, but it's not always the case.
>
> Take Kevin Garnett, who the Minnesota Timberwolves drafted straight out of high school in 1995. Minnesota management had serious trepidations about how Garnett would adjust to suddenly being surrounded by grown men in their twenties and thirties instead of his high school friends.
>
> Flip Saunders, the Timberwolves coach at the time, told Wertheim what the team was thinking: "Lots of other guys on the team had families and kids. Are they going to want to hang out with an eighteen-year-old, and vice versa?"

But much to the Timberwolves' surprise, Garnett arrived with a fairly large peer group, all of whom lived with Garnett. According to Wertheim, Garnett later credited them for keeping him grounded and helping him thrive as a player.

However, there will always be a few, friends and family alike, who think that when you make it big, you owe them a piece of your success. They're the ones Petkac calls the "Not Sure How I Got Here, But I'm Going to Milk It for All It's Worth" guys. They're the hangers on, the unofficial bodyguards, the quasi–financial advisors who seem to suck up extra cash and run up ridiculous tabs on the athlete's dime. They're one reason former NBA baller Metta World Peace (previously known as Ron Artest) nearly went broke after the first two years of his career. He told L. Jon Wertheim of *Sports Illustrated*, "Probably wasted a couple of million or so. It seemed like the right thing to do. I wanted to take care of my friends."

There's nothing wrong with wanting to hook your friends up if you come into some money, especially if most of you come from the same background or neighborhood and have been hanging out, playing against each other, and eating at each other's houses as long as you can remember. And certainly there's something admirable about wanting to care for your family when you start making good money: paying off your mom's house, buying your brother a car to replace the beater he's been driving, and so on. There is nothing wrong with that, as long as you keep it under control.

However, some friends, and even cousins and other family, will inevitably come swimming around like leeches the moment you have money. They will try to make you feel like they are entitled to a piece of the pie because of your good fortune, and if you don't immediately pay their credit card bill, let them crash at your house indefinitely, or pick up the $4,000 tab at the club, they'll guilt trip you, insisting that you've gotten a swollen head and have forgotten where you came from. The trouble is, the guilt trip *works*.

"The biggest thing I've heard some players say is that the hardest thing for them is to say no to family and friends," says Mike Golic. "I knew players who were paying for the houses of three family members, buying cars, and the whole deal. Guys spend a ton of money helping their friends and family live the lifestyle they're living.

THE "BLACK TAX"

Among African Americans, this is known as the "black tax," and it's not limited to professional sports. In fact, among professionals of color in many fields, from business to medicine, there's an unspoken expectation that if you're making good money, you're obligated to share the wealth. Sheena Allen, founder and CEO of fintech company CapWay, tweeted, "Many Blacks in my peer group are making good money but because they're the first person in their family to 'make it,' they are still living paycheck-to-paycheck because their money isn't just their money. Their money is mom's light bill money, little bro's football money, etc."

But while cultural pressure to become everyone's benefactor might be more prevalent in the African American community, nearly all pro athletes have to deal with people who come to them palms up. If they're good guys who care about the people in their lives, they might pull out their wallet or checkbook. And if a few of those people looking for money are unscrupulous, addicted, lazy, or just bad with money, a few one-time handouts can become an exploitative relationship that makes it difficult for you to build wealth because, despite making a six- or seven-figure income, you're living paycheck to paycheck and don't understand why.

Here's a good general rule: never loan money to friends and family because most of the time, they won't pay it back. That can ruin your relationships. If you really want to help out someone you care about, find out the bare minimum they need to solve their problem and give them a grant. Make it clear that they never have to pay you back but that they're also not getting another cent out of you.

THE DANGERS OF TRUSTING THE WRONG PEOPLE

There's a maxim I like to share with my professional athlete clients:

The people you trusted most before you started making money are the people you should trust the least to help you manage that money.

That might seem a little harsh, but money changes people, and the ones closest to you are no exceptions. Some may want to help you with your finances once you become successful and have the best of intentions, but if they're not professionals in the field, they will cause you more harm than good. Your father might offer to help with your investments or insist that you sit down with the nice woman who's prepared his and your mother's taxes for twenty years, and that's very kind. A guy you grew up with and lived next to since you were seven years old might say that since he got his associate's degree in accounting at community college, he'd be glad to handle your bookkeeping until you get settled, and he could be totally sincere.

This is why I recommend to athletes that they set up a businesslike organizational structure with a CMO, CFO, and COO running the show. Those people are there to help you protect yourself from bad advice and interference, even from people with good intentions, while you're busy traveling, training, competing, and earning a living.

Even the people you trust can get you in trouble if they aren't licensed specialists. The finances of a professional athlete can be incredibly complex, and even good people can give in to temptation. Former Los Angeles Kings hockey player Jack Johnson was forced to declare bankruptcy in 2014 after his own mother and father took out millions of dollars in loans in their son's name—loans they couldn't repay. Over the next few years, most of Johnson's $4.4 million salary went to repay those loans. I'll bet that was a tense Thanksgiving table.

And of course, there's the other kind of person: the cousin who's never been able to hold down a job, the pal of a pal whom you played against in high school and who always seems to have a side hustle, the ex-girlfriend who's so eager to "get together and talk" now that you're flush. Money brings out the worst in some people, and becoming their benefactor will invite an element into your life that brings you nothing but trouble. Writing for *Propeller* magazine, Jonah Hall relates the wisdom of NBA great Charles Barkley on this topic: "Barkley's simple advice for young athletes: 'You've got to learn to get rid of your family and friends who are freeloaders.' Barkley's one reference point is Dr. Phil, who tells America that giving people money doesn't solve all money problems. Perfect. All wrapped up. If you're an athlete, as soon as you become a professional, forget about everyone around you whom you are mildly suspicious of. Keep all your money, and live in an isolated bubble in which people are unnecessary."

Or to quote NFL superstar Marshawn Lynch from a memorable January 2020 press conference, "Take care of y'all's chicken," meaning money. Look after your money and your well-being because not everybody has your best interests at heart:

- NFL Hall of Fame receiver Art Monk lost $50,000 to a scheme hatched by his former teammate, Terry Orr, who convinced several ex-teammates to invest in his failing shoe company but used the cash to pay off personal debts.

- In the ESPN documentary *Broke*, former Cleveland Browns star quarterback Bernie Kosar admitted that he had lost a fortune by making the terrible mistake of allowing his father to manage his money. Dad made wretched investments, and Kosar's losses were huge. But beyond that, the QB admitted that he had been unable to say no to friends and family who came to him for handouts and had given away so much money over the years that he didn't even know how much he was down. Ouch.

- When number-three draft pick Trent Richardson signed a four-year, $20.5 million contract with the Cleveland Browns in 2012, he bought a house for himself ($850,000) and one for his grandmother in Florida ($350,000). But what killed him was neglecting his finances. It wasn't until 2015 that he finally reviewed his accounts, and he found that his friends and family members had been having fun at his expense. Among other things, they had charged him for bottle service at bars, bought stuff on Amazon using his account, and paid for eleven Netflix and eight Hulu accounts in his name. Richardson found that his "loved ones" had burned through a total of $1.6 million of his money in just ten months in 2015.

It may sound impossible that a few friends and a few Netflix accounts could wreak such financial havoc, but it's not if you think about the collective impact of constant reckless spending, especially when it's invisible because you're not keeping track of what goes out and carefully monitoring your account balances. A little thought experiment reveals the potential scope of the problem.

Let's say you have seven friends and family members who make a habit of treating you like you have a bottomless bank account. For those seven friends, because you're a good guy who likes being generous, you regularly do the following:

- Give them cash
- Pay their credit card balances
- Pick up the check at fancy restaurants and high-end clubs
- Pay for online purchases
- Pick up the tab for Netflix, Amazon Prime, HBO, and other entertainment
- Cover the cost of things they insist they can't afford, like smartphones, laptops, plane tickets, and designer clothes

Suppose you float each of these seven people an average of $500 a month in cash, and in any given month, you spend $2,000 covering their credit card balances. You take some or all of them out to eat six times a month with an average bill of $350. You've given them your Amazon account password so they can buy what they need, and they do—to the tune of $800 a month. You burn an average of $400 per month on merchandise, and as for Netflix, Prime, and HBO Max—those add up to $308 each month.

In a year, that's $73,296. If you're making LeBron James money, that's petty cash. But you're probably not making that kind of money. If you're a young MLB player making about $600,000 (which is around what you'll make for your first three years, until you're eligible for arbitration), you're probably only taking home about $300,000. That means you're spending around a quarter of your net income on leeches and freeloaders who have probably never offered to pay you back. And these are conservative numbers.

TIME-OUT

One simple way to prevent your bank account from being bled dry: *never* give anyone access to your financial information or e-commerce accounts. No giving out credit or debit card numbers and security codes. No sharing bank account numbers and routing numbers. No providing buddies with your usernames and passwords for Amazon, Alibaba, Netflix, Hulu, social media, or anything else. It's not just that they might abuse the information but also that they might make it easy for someone else to steal. What can happen? Well, a few years ago, an NBA superstar had his credit card number stolen online and the thieves used it to spend more than $500,000 on diamonds, Vespa scooters, Cadillacs, and casino gambling. There are some sketchy people out there; you don't want them anywhere close to your personal financial information.

THE "OH, SHIT!" INDEX

It doesn't even take identity thieves or grifting friends to cost you hundreds of thousands of dollars. It can be as simple as you being a generous person and wanting to take care of people, and maybe wanting to show off your success *just* a little bit.

These are some extremely common scenarios that can end up being very, very expensive. I've ranked them according to what I call the "Oh, Shit" Index (OSI for polite company) because that's what you say when you finally look at your checking account balance or credit card statement after a month of doing some of these things. My rankings:

"OH, SHIT" RANKING	RESULT
1	You slap yourself and vow never to let things get this out of hand again.
2	You transfer money between accounts and send some "WTF?" texts to your crew.
3	Some automatic payments default, you receive a few collections calls, and you get into a few fights with soon-to-be-ex-friends.
4	You freak out, panic, and wonder if you'll be able to make your mortgage this month.

Now, let's take a look at some common choices well-to-do pro athletes commonly make regarding their friends and family members and see where they fall on the OSI:

You buy a six-bedroom, fifteen-thousand-square-foot house even though it's just you so your crew can hang there pretty much 24-7.

"Oh, shit!"

4

Why: Because you're taking on a huge mortgage debt for a house you don't need and supporting what are essentially renters who pay no rent.

You're always throwing expensive parties because you have the big house, and your buddies always wind up inviting five times as many people as you originally intended.

"Oh, shit!"

3

Why: Because you end up footing the bill for food and drink for hundreds of people, can sustain damage to your property, and risk having the police called, which damages your brand.

When you and your friends and their significant others go out, you always pick up the tab.

"Oh, shit!"

2

You buy top-of-the-line clothes, watches, cars, and other lifestyle accessories, spending far more than you need to, because that's just what guys in your sport do. You feel like you have to compete with your fellow athletes.

"Oh, shit!"

4

Why: Because this is how athletes get trapped in massive debt: $30,000 Patek Philippe or Audemars Piguet watches, a small fleet of Bentleys, BMWs, and Teslas, $5,000 handmade suits you wear a few times, even $2,500 Tom Ford sunglasses.

You take your crew and their girlfriends/wives to Vegas, the Final Four, Miami, Hawaii, all on your dime.

"Oh, shit!"

3

Why: These might not be frequent trips, but they're expensive. Airfare, hotels, event or show tickets, bodyguards, and of course food and drink. Fly everyone first class and stay at the Four Seasons and you're talking $50,000 for a long weekend. And such travel is a liability nightmare.

You're constantly bailing your friends out of jams—paying their debts, getting them out of jail, and lending them cash when they're strapped.

"Oh, shit!"

1

Why: You're pissing away your hard-earned money taking care of adults who should be able to take care of their own affairs.

THE FRIENDS AND FAMILY PLAN

Don't let my suspicions turn you off from taking financial advice from close family and friends who really care about you. Some of the best common sense, formative financial advice you'll ever get comes from family, especially when you're young and it shapes how you look at money and goals for the rest of your life.

"I wasn't raised in a family where there was a lot of money," says Solomon Wilcots. "My dad helped us to understand the value of real estate and investment over time, and most of it was through purchasing and selling land over time. My dad is a Baptist minister. He owns two hundred and fifty acres outside of Jackson, Mississippi, and raised cattle. My mom and my dad, neither one of them ever went to college, but they're financially strong. They're good. They don't require their kids to take care of them or supplement their income."

For those less well-meaning friends and family members, here are some fixes. This is my version of Verizon's Friends and Family Plan. It starts with two commitments from you. First, you must immediately begin the search for your Board of Directors, hire them as quickly as possible, and put them in charge of all your finances. Second, commit to ending any unstructured financial support of family members and friends, even close family like parents and siblings. No more enabling their reckless lifestyles.

Notice that I said *unstructured*. I'm not suggesting that you stop helping the people you care about, especially if you're blessed with the talent and good fortune to be making millions of dollars a year while they're struggling. What I am suggesting is that your financial assistance be structured, tracked, and controlled. No more handing out cash. No more picking up the bill for everything. No more making it rain.

Once you make those commitments, there are many ways you can continue to offer financial support to the people who need it without letting this spending get out of control. One simple way to help is to establish a policy with whomever needs regular support: you'll pay them a set amount every month and not a penny more. Even better, have your attorney write up a contract to cover this arrangement and include an "out" clause: if they ask you for more money than the agreed-upon amount, they are immediately and permanently cut off.

You could also do what some other pro athletes have done: give friends and family prepaid debit cards, reloading them each month with a set amount. Everyone gets the same amount, no exceptions. If someone burns through the card balance by the fifteenth, too bad. Yes, some people in your life will lash out at you for having a swollen head and forgetting where you came from. Let them. Those people don't care about you, just your money.

There are also ways to help friends and family without giving them cash. One way is to pay off some of their outstanding debts. This is a go-to move for many athletes who get big contracts or signing bonuses. After Kansas City Royals prospect Brady Singer went eighteenth in the 2018 MLB draft and received a $4.25 million signing bonus, he recorded a YouTube video in which he told his stunned parents he was paying off their mortgage and all their other debts. Consider paying off someone's mortgage, credit card, car loan, or student loan debt. You'll maintain control of your spending while giving them the gift of freedom.

Finally, consider investing in a retirement plan for someone. You can open a traditional or Roth IRA for a friend or family member and even contribute to it every year as long as you adhere to the contribution limits. You'll want to run this past your CFO, but imagine giving a friend who's in his twenties a nest egg that can grow for forty years and become something he can build on for his future. It's not glamorous, but it lasts way longer than bottle service. Just one thing—prior to setting up any arrangement with friends or family, have your CFO design and approve the plan. It needs to fit within *your* plan.

Be selective about whom you offer help to. You're not a bank. You're not obligated to give financial support to everyone who comes along, no matter what they say. You worked your ass off to get where you are, and while you may feel that you owe a debt to your mom and dad or a beloved coach, you don't owe anyone else. So when somebody approaches you with their hand out, ask yourself some questions. Is this person trying to manipulate you into helping them? Are they suggesting they are entitled to some of your money? Is this someone who's borrowed money before but never paid it back? Are they a perpetual screwup who can't hold a job and is always getting into trouble? Worse, is the person a criminal or an addict? If the answers to any of those questions is yes, then walk away.

KNOW THE SCORE

Retailers, fashion designers, automakers, liquor brands and bars definitely saw professional athletes coming when they set their prices. Young and recently rich? Check. Status conscious? Check. Eager to impress friends and dates? Check. Still, you should know how you're getting ripped off by ridiculous markups on luxury items. Then if you still choose to lay down the card, at least you know what you're getting into.

CATEGORY	COMMON MARKUP (SOURCE)
Designer apparel	Up to 1,200% (Oliver Cabell)
Designer accessories	Up to 2,000% (Oliver Cabell)
iPhone 11	300% (CNBC)

Cristal champagne	1,000%+ (LasVegasNightclubs.com)
Luxury beauty products	700% (Beautyindepedent.com)
Diamonds	50–200% (TheStreet.com)
Luxury cars	20% dealer markup (*Washington Post*)

YOUR ENTOURAGE RULE BOOK

Ideally, your goal should be to prevent money conflicts and losses *before* they happen. Some of the issues you've read about wind up shattering friendships and driving a wedge between family members, and nobody wants that. Smart athletes set clear boundaries with their friends and with anyone in their social circle—friends of friends. To help you with that, I've put together this "Entourage Rule Book." I know, you probably don't have an entourage, but I had to call it something. Whether they're your buddies, your crew, your homeboys, or just "the guys," make sure everyone knows these rules ahead of time and follows them to the letter. No exceptions.

Instructions: As early as possible in your career—certainly, as soon as you sign your big contract or land your first big prize purse—make sure all your close friends and family members know these rules and know you're serious about enforcing them. Exercise discretion about applying them to your parents and significant other or spouse, for obvious reasons.

Rule #1: Everyone signs a nondisclosure agreement (NDA) before they can come back to your place.

You won't want to make your buddies do this, and some of them will be mad about it, but stick to your guns. This one is nonoptional. If they don't sign, they don't walk through the door. Anyone they bring whom you don't know has to sign an NDA too. Remember, be the good cop: "Guys, it's not my rule; it's my attorney's rule."

An NDA prohibits anyone who signs it from revealing anything they heard, saw, or photographed under the circumstances specified in the agreement—in this case, at your house. If they post sensitive photos on Instagram or tell their friends about so-and-so getting drunk and passing out in the pool, you can take legal action against them. Your brand is valuable, and you need to safeguard it from rumor, social media misunderstandings, and potential lawsuits.

Logistically, this is easy. Have your lawyer draw up an NDA and put it on DocuSign, and then either you or your security guys have it available on a phone or iPad for guests to read. They sign with their finger, screenshot their ID, and they're in. Make sure the folks on your Board of Directors always have the NDA on their phones too.

Rule #2: No social media posts about the stuff you do.

Think about LeBron. You ever see him on Instagram in degenerate mode, getting crazy at the strip club? No. Why? Because he's a smart man and a savvy entrepreneur. He knows he's a billion-dollar brand and he cannot afford to let some random post on social media wreck that. He may well be partying hard enough to throw the earth off its axis, but whatever he's doing, it stays *private*. That's what you want.

Nobody is allowed to post anything about their time hanging with you without your written approval via email or text. I don't care how innocent it might seem. I don't care if it's you singing "Happy Birthday" to your ninety-year-old grandma. Give friends one strike, as long as it's an innocent gaffe. We're all so accustomed to posting and tweeting *everything* these days that they might forget. But after that, if they stumble again, they don't hang with you anymore.

Rule #3: No uninvited guests.

Friends and family don't bring someone to your house for a party or any other event without you having approved the person. They have to submit names and identification to you at least twenty-four hours in advance, and your team runs a background check on each person. If the guest doesn't have any serious issues and they're willing to sign your NDA, they're good to go. But if they've got multiple arrests or are on the sex offender list, forget it.

This also means you're going to have to turn away last-second drop-ins. The old "Man, I brought Carlos along at the last second and forgot; he's a good guy—could you let him in this one time?" isn't going to fly. That person doesn't get in, no matter how inconvenient it is. You'll call an Uber for him, but otherwise, it's nighty night. This is why it's good to have security; you don't have to be the bad guy.

Rule #4: When you go out, there's a hard cap on what you'll spend on the group. After that, everyone pays their own way.
This helps you avoid that "Oh, shit!" moment when you see a $7,000 bill after a big night out and want to pass out. Text everybody before you all arrive at the restaurant or club, "Guys, my cap for tonight is $1,500. See you all there!" Your friends already know that after you've dropped $1,500, they can't ask you to spend another cent.

When you're out, just take your waiter or bartender aside, inform him or her that you'll be picking up the first $1,500 (or whatever number you choose) of the bill and you'd like him or her to inform you when the total gets close to that number. When it does, you just tell the table, "Guys, just so you're aware, I'm capped." They'll all know that from this point on, anything they order comes out of their pocket. Get the bill, sign it, and close it out. Now, start a new running tab that doesn't have your card attached to it.

Of course, you can choose to go past your night's cap. It's your money. But I would advise against doing that very often. If people think the cap is optional, they won't respect it. Enforce it 95 percent of the time, and save the 5 percent for a very special occasion.

Enforcing the rules isn't fun, but you know what's less fun? Being broke. Your real friends will understand what you're trying to do, because they care about you. The hangers-on and leeches who just want to have a good time on your dime will pitch a fit, but who cares? You don't want those people in your life anyway.

One last thing about friends: your employees are *not* your friends. I told you not to hire friends and family for your Board of Directors, and that's not just because they lack the expertise and training you need.

It's also because at some point, you may need to fire them. That's why everyone who works for you also has to sign an NDA before they start.

Your employees might genuinely like you, but watch how fast things can change if things go south, personally or professionally. If you're forced to part ways with a member of your financial team, you don't want your ex-CFO or accountant roaming around spreading ugly rumors about you to your sponsors. You have a lot to lose now, so it's time to act that way. The real professionals, like your real friends, will understand and respect your game.

OVERTIME

The "Friend Or Leech?" Quiz

Is the person you're hanging with a friend who genuinely wants to spend time with you or a leech who just wants to sponge cash off you and get you to pay for everything? Take this quick test to find out. Just answer "yes" or "no" to each question and assess the score at the bottom.

1. Does the person give you a hard time about signing your NDA?

[YES | NO]

2. Does the person seem to expect you to pay for everything?

[YES | NO]

3. Does the person ask for loans and not pay them back on time?

[YES | NO]

4. Does the person crash at your place without offering to cover some of the costs?

[YES | NO]

5. Does the person always seem to be short on cash?

[YES | NO]

6. Is the person always asking you to put money into one "opportunity" or another?

[YES | NO]

7. Does the person come to you with money questions even though you've made it clear you have a financial chain of command?

[YES | NO]

8. Does the person have a history of job losses, criminal activity or substance abuse?

[YES | NO]

SCORING

6–8 "yes" answers	Leech. Cut this loser loose.
4–5 "yes" answers	Possible leech. Beware. Give this person a very short leash.
2–3 "yes" answers	"Training wheels" friend who may have to be taught the ropes before he or she earns your trust.
0–1 "yes" answers	Friend.

CHAPTER FIVE

LIVE LIKE YOU HAVE A LOT TO LOSE . . . BECAUSE YOU DO

We all know about the famous cautionary tales, iconic athletes like Tiger Woods and Mike Tyson whose character flaws led them to flame out as spectacularly as they rose to fame and fortune. But there are many, many more stories of athletes who had everything but whose questionable character, bad decision-making, and toxic social circle ruined them. Consider these men (and one woman) as examples *not* to emulate:

- **Kareem Hunt.** Hunt was the main running back for the Kansas City Chiefs through the 2018 season, but on November 30, 2018, after the gossip website TMZ published video showing him shoving and punching a woman, the Chiefs released him. He lost most of the 2019 season due to a suspension by the NFL and hernia surgery and then signed with the Browns as a free agent in 2020. Hunt's career now seems to be bouncing back, but he definitely lost some opportunities, including a Super Bowl ring with the Chiefs.

- **Ryan Leaf.** There was a time when there was serious debate over whether the Indianapolis Colts should select Ryan Leaf or Peyton Manning with the first pick in the 1998 NFL draft. Fortunately for the Colts, they went with Manning, because the San Diego Chargers got a lot more than they bargained for with the talented but out-of-control Leaf. He behaved erratically, showed a poor work ethic, played poorly, and feuded with players and coaches. After retiring at twenty-six, Leaf had problems with drug addiction, pleading guilty to felony burglary and drug possession in Montana, serving two years before his release in December of 2014. Sadly, while I was writing this, Leaf was arrested on a domestic battery charge. Just a tragedy.

- **Michael Vick.** Unless you lived on a deserted island back in 2007, you knew Vick's story. An incredibly gifted quarterback out of Virginia Tech, he played six stellar seasons with the Atlanta Falcons, but in 2007 it was discovered that he was involved in the illegal sport of dog fighting. The Falcons released him, he spent twenty-one months in prison, and public revulsion toward dog fighting ensured that his career would never regain its previous glitter. He wound up declaring bankruptcy in 2008, and then bounced around from the Philadelphia Eagles to the New York Jets to the Pittsburgh Steelers before retiring in 2017.

- **Johnny Manziel.** Manziel was a Heisman winner and a can't-miss quarterback coming out of Texas A&M, but even before he was out of college, he was running afoul of the law, fighting with his teammates, and violating NCAA rules about accepting money. Once he got into the NFL, he was a shit show, getting in fights, missing practices, getting in more trouble with the law, and allegedly using drugs. His marketing firm and sports agent both fired him, and he wound up being chased out of the NFL, played in the Canadian Football League for a while, and now spends his time playing golf.

- **Adam "Pac-Man" Jones.** Jones was a star cornerback for the Tennessee Titans when he went to a Las Vegas strip club in February 2007. He'd already had issues with alleged drug possession, disorderly conduct, and assault, but in Vegas things escalated. Jones and some other players "made it rain" cash in the club, and in the scramble to retrieve the money, a security guard was shot and paralyzed. Jones was charged with felony coercion, battery, and threat to life and later sued by two injured security guards and ordered to pay them a total of $12.3 million. Run-ins with the law continued for Jones for years, and in 2008, his house went into foreclosure.

- **Hope Solo**. Women aren't immune to bad behavior. For years on the US Women's Soccer Team, Solo was a menacing presence in the goal and a sports icon. But she fought with coaches, leveled verbal broadsides at teammates, lashed out on social media, leaked unsavory pictures of herself online, and in 2014 was arrested on domestic assault charges. In 2016, when she attacked the Swedish national team that had beaten the US women in the Olympics, she was cut from the team. A sad way for the career of one of the most decorated, admired women's soccer players in history to end.

- **Lenny Dykstra.** "Nails" was a force to be reckoned with on the field with the New York Mets and Philadelphia Phillies, but off the field he was a train wreck. His attempt to run a high-end car wash ended in multiple lawsuits. He tried to flip NHL superstar Wayne Gretzky's former house but lost it to a lienholder. By 2009 he was bankrupt, living out of his car and in hotel lobbies, and had hocked his World Series ring. I won't even go into the other felonies and legal troubles in which Dykstra found himself embroiled, except to say that in 2007 he was also named in the Mitchell Report as a steroid user.

That's just scratching the surface, too. I could talk about Ray Rice, Aaron Hernandez, Latrell Sprewell, and on and on. There are plenty of stories of pro athletes who, if they had found some way to stay on the straight and narrow, could have enjoyed long careers and great wealth. But that's the lesson of this chapter:

Your conduct and character have a powerful influence on your wealth.

WITH GREAT POWER COMES GREAT RESPONSIBILITY

We know that not all professional athletes are multimillionaires, but the public assumes that most successful professional athletes are much wealthier than the average lawyer, physician, or CEO. True or not, that means your words and actions will be under a lot more scrutiny—not just from the press but also from any private citizen with a smartphone and social media account. You're visible and relatively well-known, and that can make you a target.

Just as importantly, your public image determines the value of your brand, and your brand determines what your long-term income will be. In military science, there's a thing called a "force multiplier," a factor that allows an individual or unit to be more effective with it than without it. For example, an aircraft carrier is a spectacular force multiplier. Well, your brand is the force multiplier for your income as an athlete.

Let's say you play soccer and you sign a five-year, $15 million contract with the Portland Timbers of the MLS. Nice. You're only going to see about $7.5 million of that money because of taxes, commissions, and expenses, but suppose you also have a strong personal brand. You're charismatic, have a great sense of humor, give back to the community, and a good guy. You turn your success as a player into endorsements, speaking engagements, licensed products, brand ambassadorships, media gigs, and business opportunities that might be worth $75 million over the next ten years. You've increased your potential income by 500 percent by building and safeguarding a strong personal brand.

I hate to keep going back to Conor McGregor, but he's a fantastic example of what branding can do for you. Yes, he's a terrific fighter, but the reason he has a net worth of around $120 million is because of his style, his billionaire strut in the octagon, his personality, and his business acumen. People know who he is and what he stands for, and he knows his audience: mostly men who are cool with a little of the "bad boy" persona. He's a living master class in how to make yourself into an icon.

Remember, being a professional athlete carries a great deal of prestige; people will admire you and bring you opportunities just because of what you do. That gives you the ability to build a post-career life and income that far surpasses what you do in your sport—but only if you take care of your brand. As we saw with the examples above, bad behavior, poor choices, addiction, and illegality will ruin your brand, squander any goodwill you've built up, and leave you bankrupt and humiliated. You have a lot to lose, and the best way to keep it is to follow the following three rules:

- **Rule #1:** After your athletic ability, your personal conduct is the second most critical piece of your financial and life success and should be treated with care and respect.

- **Rule #2:** In public, always assume someone is watching.

- **Rule #3:** Erect guardrails to keep you on the straight and narrow.

LEAVE NOTHING TO CHANCE

The key mental step in following all three of those rules is to accept that once you're a successful pro athlete, you can't be as easygoing and spur-of-the-moment as maybe you used to be. Start thinking like a businessperson, because you are a business. This doesn't mean you can't have fun; you just need to be more conscious about how that fun will look to the public, how likely it is to get out of hand, what crowd it puts you into contact with, and what the downstream consequences might be.

Athletes are young. If you're young, single, and making good money, you want to have a good time with your friends. If you look at case after case of young, rich, male pro athletes getting into trouble with the law and/or his spouse, patterns start to emerge. There are lots of strip clubs, car accidents, and alcohol. So wouldn't it make sense to avoid those things if you're trying to keep your nose clean? Yes, but people don't always make wise decisions, especially when there's peer pressure to go out, cut loose, and spend big.

Fortunately, you don't have to depend solely on your own self-control and decision-making. You have a Board of Directors to help you. The most successful pro athletes with the best personal brands leave nothing to chance. They work with their Board of Directors and second-tier professionals to set up guardrails: habits, schedules, and rules that keep them on the right path. You should do the same. Here's what I mean:

- If you have someone who provides personal security for you, give him permission to police your behavior and steer you away from certain environments and situations that you've agreed on beforehand. It's your bodyguard as your conscience, sitting on your shoulder and keeping you out of the casino.

- Stick to healthy, beneficial routines that you were into before your career took off. For example, if you were a regular churchgoer before going pro and still enjoy going, then put that on your calendar for every Sunday morning and go. Anything that grounds you is a positive.

- Give yourself a realistic curfew, especially during the most hectic time in your sport's season. It doesn't have to be draconian—you don't have to be in bed by nine o'clock—but there's nothing wrong with being home by eleven, is there? The reality is, few good things happen after two in the morning. When you read stories about athletes who were arrested for assault, DUI, or disorderly conduct, a lot of them seem to occur in the wee hours. That's when people are just leaving casinos and clubs, wound up and liquored up. Avoid that scene. Set a curfew, put a reminder on your phone, and give your business manager permission to call and harass you about it if you're not home. *Note: This does not apply when you're on vacation. I'm not a monster.*

- Take up a calming, mindful discipline like meditation or yoga. There's a term for what happens when a bunch of young, rich, hot male athletes get together for a wild night on the town: "testosterone poisoning." The night's active, adrenaline is flowing, you're hyped up, one thing leads to another, and before you know it, you're taking a swing at somebody (or the other way around) and you end up in jail while the story ends up on TMZ and ESPN. It's in your best interest to calm any hot temper or impulsive behavior you may have before it can sabotage you, and meditation and yoga are terrific tools for doing that.

  Mediation has been scientifically proven to help athletes make faster decisions in pressure situations. In her book *The Sharp Solution,* brain scientist Heidi Hanna writes, "Skilled chess players and elite athletes have taught themselves to analyze complex situations more quickly in order to respond in the best way, as fast as possible." Meditation fuels that quick analysis, improves concentration and mindfulness, and is also incredible for staying cool and not reacting to provocation. Hire a meditation coach or download the Headspace or Calm app and try it out.

  As for yoga, it's definitely not just for women. If you've ever done a session of hatha yoga (one of the most popular forms), you know that by the end you're swimming in sweat and exhausted. But for athletes, yoga is the fountain of youth. It's wonderful for improving your flexibility, balance, and core strength, and its deep breathing discipline is also incredibly calming.

- Use apps like Daily Budget to track your spending and set limits for yourself. I find that when the money runs out, so does the fun. You can also contact all the banks that have issued debit cards to you and request that they put a daily point of sale limit on each card. For example, if you have a $2,000 daily point of sale limit on a card, that prevents anyone (including you) from spending more than $2,000 on that card in a day in an environment where someone is running your card in real time, like a bar or restaurant. Sure, you can call your bank and lift the limit if you want, but the hard cap makes you stop and think.

RISK-FIRST THINKING

A few years ago, ESPN's *Sport Science* ran an experiment where they tried to determine the Greatest of All Time (GOAT) among professional athletes. They compared the best-ever from a wide range of sports in metrics like strength, power, speed, finesse, quickness, reaction time, endurance, durability, pressure performances, dominance, versatility, and the difficulty of their sport. In the end, Bo Jackson got the edge over Michael Jordan as the greatest athlete ever.

If you're not old enough to remember Bo Jackson, get on YouTube and watch some video. The guy wasn't human. He was so fast, so powerful, so coordinated, and so smart that compared to him, grown men looked like boys. The trouble with Bo was that he wanted to be a two-sport athlete, and from an investment perspective, this decision represented a misunderstanding of risk versus reward.

Every level of risk comes with a potential reward. Usually, the higher the risk, the higher the potential reward. However, higher risk also comes with greater potential for loss. On the upside, there was incredible value to Bo's brand in being a superstar two-sport athlete when such a thing was (as it still is) extremely rare. Being a crossover star in MLB and the NFL was worth millions in endorsements and free press coverage. On the downside, he had twice the potential of getting injured and ending his career prematurely. A fastball to the wrist or a blown knee ligament on a cutback is bad enough for an athlete's earning power, but does courting both at the same time really make sense?

Bo and his representatives probably should have considered his options like this:

- **Option A:** Play both sports at the same time, build a one-of-a-kind brand, and be a unique superstar. Injury risk: Relatively high. Financial upside: Staggering. Risk-reward: Risk-heavy. Brand potential: Huge.

- **Option B:** Play one sport, build a superstar brand in it, and be extremely successful. Injury risk: Average. Financial upside: High. Risk-reward: Moderate. Brand potential: Moderate.

- **Option C:** Play both sports for one or two seasons, then quit one and play the other. Injury risk: Slightly above average. Financial upside: Extremely high. Risk-reward: Moderate. Brand potential: Huge.

From a risk perspective, the option to play baseball and football full-time contained too much *volatility*. Yes, the upside was extraordinary, but the chance of the opportunity ending suddenly due to injury was also unacceptably high. Option C is the best choice, a middle road that would have let Bo Jackson establish himself as a two-sport stud and build a legendary brand and then immediately lower his injury risk by walking away from either the NFL (the better choice) or MLB.

Bo could have been a twenty-year superstar in either baseball or the NFL, made tens of millions of dollars in salary (big money for the late eighties and early nineties), made hundreds of millions more from endorsements and licensing deals, and driven off into the sunset in a gold-plated Maybach automobile. But in trying to play both sports, he exposed himself to unnecessary risk. And in 1991, while playing for the LA Raiders, he sustained a severe hip injury and was never the same. By 1994, both his careers were over.

Of course, it's easy to Monday morning quarterback. Bo Jackson remains an icon, still beloved, still quite successful in media and philanthropy and other pursuits. So he did something right after all. But if he and his team looked at the risks and rewards differently, he might have capitalized on far more of his once-in-a-generation athleticism and charisma. In finance, risk is defined as the chance that the actual performance of an investment will differ from the expected performance of that investment. We measure risk in terms of *uncertainty*, and the more uncertain the outcome of an investment is, the more we demand a higher potential return to compensate for that uncertainty. Take US Treasury bonds. Even with the economic upheaval surrounding the coronavirus pandemic, they are still considered one of the safest investments in the world because they're backed by the full faith and credit of the US government. That also means they offer a low return, recently between 1 and 2 percent per year. Low risk equals low return. But the chance of losing your money is practically zero.

Hedge funds are at the opposite end of the spectrum. They are private investment funds typically available only to high net worth individuals, and they often invest in more exotic, nontraditional securities that I won't go into here. On the upside that means hedge funds can offer extraordinary potential rates of return. One study by economists from NYU and Yale found that over a six year period, the average annual return for offshore hedge funds was 13.6 percent, roughly double what you could expect from investing in the broader market. However, that high return also comes with higher risk. Because you have to risk a lot of capital to invest in a hedge fund, if it loses value, you can lose a great deal of money. High return equals high risk.

KNOW THE SCORE

If you want to cut loose and be smart, bring the party home, where you have total control of the environment. Love the idea of treating your buddies to a high-end liquor tasting, but don't want to be hassled by autograph seekers at a bar? Hire a top-flight bartender. Want to go to Vegas but hate the security issues? Hire a company to throw a casino night at your place! Dying to get to the club but hate the crowds? Hire a top DJ with a lighting package and turn your house into a private club. Make sure everybody signs your NDA, have some discreet security, hire professional bartenders to cut people off who appear loaded, and make sure everyone who needs an Uber gets one. Invite your neighbors so you don't have to worry about the noise. That's how the pros party safely!

THE RISK EQUATION

Your behavior impacts your paycheck. If you take more risks or have a very public lifestyle, you might find yourself paying more for insurance—especially for a liability umbrella policy—or simply unable to get coverage. Insurers want to know whom they're insuring. Teams are the same way. That may not matter when you're at the top of your game, but it does when you've gotten older and your team is trying to decide if they want you around or not.

Irresponsible behavior can shorten careers. On the flip side, athletes with good character don't give their team a reason to cut them. With the minimum salary in the NBA over one million dollars a year now, a couple of extra seasons can really make a difference in retirement.

If behavior and character could be worth millions, I think you'll agree it's smart to begin assessing your off-the-field or off-the-court behavior in terms of risk versus reward, in the same way an investor assesses an investment in terms of risk versus return. You should be doing this because your behavior away from your sport affects your brand, and your brand is a vital determinant of your earning potential.

You can look at the importance of your brand this way. When you're playing, your brand might constitute as much as 40 percent of your earning potential in the form of endorsements, speaking engagements, movie and book deals, personal appearances, and the like. (If you're in a purse-based sport like tennis or triathlon, it can be as much as 80 percent.) For the typical team sports player in the NBA, NFL, MLB, NHL, or MLS, that might look like this:

PRO ATHLETE EARNING FACTORS—PRE-RETIREMENT

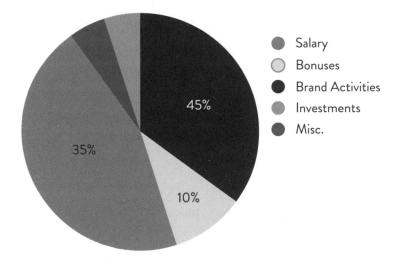

- Salary
- Bonuses
- Brand Activities
- Investments
- Misc.

45%

35%

10%

"Brand activities" are all related to how well you're liked in the community, whether you're perceived as being a good guy (or gal), and whether your public image is consistent with your private behavior. The athletes who land the lucrative shoe and gear endorsement deals aren't just the winners. They're the ones corporations and their advertising agencies want associated with their products. Nobody gives seven-figure deals to athletes who are perceived as punks, domestic abusers, or drunks. In fact, most endorsement and brand ambassadorship contracts contain "character clauses" that give the company the right to terminate the contract if the athletes says or does something that's counter to the company's values.

So protecting your brand can make you big money while you're playing. However, that's nothing compared to its importance after you're done. Unless you have deferred money in your contract, after you stop playing, your salary and bonuses stop *instantly*. Now, apart from any income you might have from investments like real estate, you're almost entirely dependent on income streams built on your brand. This is what that looks like:

PRO ATHLETE EARNING FACTORS—POSTRETIREMENT

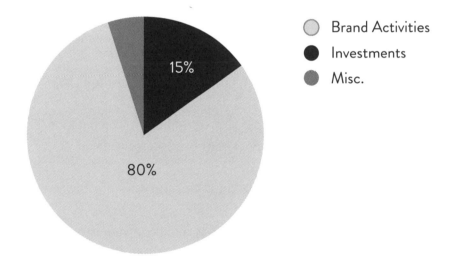

Even before you're retired, your brand and reputation will determine the size and power of your personal network, the kinds of business partnership and investment opportunities you receive, the post-career endorsement and speaking opportunities offered to you, and the types of media jobs available to you. If you want to stay in your sport as a coach or manager, whether you're able to do that or not will have a great deal to do with what other people thought of you when you were playing. Were you a team-first player? Did you listen? Were you disciplined? Those things all matter to your financial future, and they're all part of your brand. If people see you as someone who's out of control, bad tempered, irresponsible, or hypocritical, why would they want to do business with you?

If you want to build a bright future, it's time to start viewing all your activities through the prism of risk. Risk management professionals use various equations to determine risk for things like insurance policies, but I like this equation for its simplicity:

$$Probability \ x \ Consequence = Risk$$

Probability is the likelihood that something will happen on a 1–10 scale. Something that's very unlikely might only have a probability of one, while something that's certain might have a probability of ten. *Consequence* is the result of that thing happening on a scale of one to four:

- 1—A minor consequence like a parking ticket or fine from the team.

- 2—A troubling consequence that could hurt your reputation, like being kicked out of a bar or embarrassed on social media.

- 3—A serious consequence that could land you in court or the hospital.

- 4—A catastrophic consequence that could end your career or cost you all your assets or permanently damage your brand.

You can figure out those two variables easily. Let's say you're planning a road trip from Los Angeles to Las Vegas with three other teammates. Great! But you're planning to drive yourselves, which adds an element of risk, because the probability of all four of you drinking alcohol is a ten—a 100 percent chance. You're also planning to drive between different clubs and casinos, which means the more you drink, the higher the probability of an accident or DUI. Plus, you also have to drive yourselves back to Los Angeles, and that means an even higher probability of some kind of alcohol-related problem.

WHAT WITCH?

I recommend that my clients gauge risk by the "What's the Worst that Could Happen?" standard. If you're into acronyms, that's WTWTCH (pronounced "What witch?"). By the "What witch?" standard, the worst thing that could happen on this Vegas bro trip is somebody driving under the influence, and there's a 50 percent probability of that happening—a probability score of 5. Talking consequences, that means there's a fifty-fifty chance you're going to put yourself in position for a DUI or drunk and disorderly arrest (3 on the consequence scale), an accident (3), or even being charged with vehicular manslaughter (4). So, using the equation:

$$Probability\ of\ 5$$
$$x$$
$$Consequence\ of\ 3\ or\ 4$$
$$=$$
$$Risk\ of\ 15–20$$

That's dangerously high. Your risk score should always remain below a ten—ideally, below a five. The breakdown:

Low-risk activities:	1–5
Moderate risk:	6–10
High risk:	**10–15**
Stupid risk:	**15+**

I would lose my license if I ever recommended that one of my clients put their money into an investment that had a 50 percent chance of catastrophic failure! Athletes who engage in high-risk private activities without considering the potential risk to their brand, reputation, and health are guilty of the same kind of malpractice.

Does that mean you can't go to Vegas or that you can't have any fun? *Of course not.* It means you have to be smart about risk. In the risk management business, there's something called *risk mitigation*. That means you find ways to reduce risk by either lowering the probability or softening the consequences. Identify the specific threat, identify the risk it poses, and identify ways to neutralize the threat and reduce the risk. For your Vegas trip, the fix is simple: *fly in and hire a limo*. Nobody is driving, so that risk is completely eliminated.

As you consider the value of your brand and what it means to your future wealth, start looking at all the potential risks in your private activities in terms of that "What witch?" standard. Could an activity get you injured? Arrested? Sued? Humiliated on social media or in the press? I know it might seem like a buzzkill to think about risk when you just want to have fun, but as the saying goes, you can either think about it now or cry about it later.

Blatant plug time: in a few hours of bite-sized videos, my Financial Literacy for Athletes series will make you smarter about all this stuff, from risk to volatility in the stock market. Go to WealthLit101.com to sign up.

KNOW THE SCORE

If you've been active as a pro for a few years, you've got to be on top of your social media presence. These days it's a huge part of your brand, and marketers love it because with Instagram and Twitter, they don't have to guess how many fans you're reaching. They can see the real-time numbers. So you've got to be all over this stuff. My favorite tool for gauging your influence and brand value on social media is Hookit.com. Go to their rankings page and you can look up the top brands on social media in real time by sport, league, month, and even on a player or team basis. It's a great tool for tracking your social media muscle.

RISK FACTORS

Sportswriter Alex Fishkind writes, "In a modern-day world seemingly run by social media, the athletes that we once adored and idolized have become bait for scrutiny and shaming. Just as the celebrities of Hollywood and Los Angeles are followed by paparazzi relentlessly day and night, athletes of every sport are under a magnifying glass, with every move—or lack thereof—subject to criticism and critique."

Like it or not, he's right. So let's take a clear-eyed look at the major areas of risk that professional athletes need to watch out for. Some will not apply to you; that's fine. But they illustrate the reality that in today's world, where everyone is a potential reporter and bad news goes global in seconds, you've got to watch your brand and reputation like a hawk.

SEX

From former President Bill Clinton to Pittsburgh Steelers star quarterback Ben Roethlisberger, many powerful, popular individuals have been brought down by allegations of sexual misconduct. Athletes are especially at risk for obvious reasons: they're young, fit, in the public eye, and at least perceived to be rich. In other words, they have a target on their back.

That's why, in general, being a "player" is a bad idea for an athlete. At the very least, you risk unleashing a flood of anger from one-night stands on social media. At worst, you could become a victim of identity theft, physical theft, or blackmail, or have a woman show up at your door claiming you're the father of her child. So when it comes to sex, if you are going to play the field, treat every encounter with a new partner as a potential harassment or paternity lawsuit.

Use birth control, obviously. Get the person to sign the same NDA you make your friends sign. (I know, it's a mood killer, but it's also a deal breaker.) If you're going on a date, have your assistant run a quick background check before you leave. If she's got a psycho Twitter history or a criminal record, maybe . . . rain check?

If a woman you've been with says she's pregnant, insist that she get a pregnancy test from *your* doctor. If she is pregnant, insist on a paternity test. Both might seem cold, but would you rather be supporting a child who isn't yours?

Finally, if you're married, don't. Just don't. Don't screw around. Because that can only lead to . . .

DIVORCE

In his famous 2009 *Sports Illustrated* story that suggested a shockingly high number of retired NFL and NBA players were going broke, Pablo S. Torre also wrote: "In 1996, when Panthers owner Jerry Richardson . . . addressed his players, one of them asked, 'What's the most dangerous thing that could happen to us financially?' . . . Mr. Richardson said, 'Divorce.' . . . In divorce proceedings, of course, husbands routinely lose half of their net worth. But for athletes there is an aggravating factor: when the divorce happens. Most splits occur in retirement, when the player's peak earnings period is long over and making a comparable living is virtually impossible."

The *New York Times* and *Sports Illustrated* estimate that the divorce rate among pro athletes is between 60 and 80 percent, much higher than the 50 percent rate among the general public. That's not surprising. Many athletes travel a great deal and are in situations where infidelity is easy. But you only have to look at the divorces of superstars like Michael Jordan and Tiger Woods to know what a disaster marriage dissolution can be.

If you're already married when you go pro, the best advice I can give you is to stay away from temptation. Get marriage counseling to keep you and your partner in a good place, and get a teammate or someone you trust to be your wingman and keep you out of trouble. However, if you meet someone you want to marry after you're making good money, treat the marriage like what it is: a shared property agreement between two parties.

If you've signed a big contract or have the prospects of one in your future, have your attorney draw up an airtight prenuptial agreement. Signing it is mandatory; if not, the wedding is off. A mature, intelligent fiancée with good intentions will understand the need, while a predator who's only after your money will object. I know, it's not romantic, but neither is losing half your wealth in a divorce settlement.

Suppose infidelity is inevitable? I'm not judging, but you have to be smart. First of all, if you can't keep your zipper zipped, consider getting some counseling. Hire a private investigator to research anyone you're fooling around with. Have every partner sign your NDA. Most importantly keep your affairs away from your home life. No sexual dalliances in your home area code (remember what Ludacris said about area codes?). Don't give your partners your phone number; use a texting app like WhatsApp with an alternate number. Block them on social media.

Better yet, just don't screw around. It's not worth the paranoia, not to mention the legal fees.

SUBSTANCE ABUSE

From Hall of Fame linebacker Lawrence Taylor to cycling legend Lance Armstrong, the stories of athletes whose careers and lives were ruined by the use and abuse of recreational and performance-enhancing drugs (PEDs) are tragic and well-known. Hell, there's an entire generation of baseball superstars who may never make it into the Hall of Fame because of suspicions about their PED use. When it comes to PEDs, the Gateway Foundation says that pressure to stay competitive and gain a competitive advantage, as well as a "do whatever it takes" culture in sports, leads many athletes to turn to anabolic steroids, stimulants, growth hormones, and beta blockers to improve muscle growth, reduce recovery time, and calm jitters.

On the recreational side, alcohol and drugs like cocaine and opiates are common temptations for people with money to spend and a "life is a party" attitude. Just as dangerous is the misuse of opioids for pain management. According to a 2014 study published in the journal *Substance Abuse and Rehabilitation*, 52 percent of football players reported using opiates at some point in their career—and 71 percent of *those* players admit to misusing the drugs.

Obviously, drugs like marijuana, which is legal in some states, represent a gray area for athletes. You're an adult, so use your own judgment and act according to the laws in your area. Otherwise, my best advice is to avoid both recreational and performance-enhancing drugs at all costs. Most nonpot recreational drugs are illegal, and possession of them is a felony that could land you in jail (see Risks). As for PEDs, they are banned by every major sport, and virtually all sports have testing programs. Athletes discovered to be using PEDs risk suspension, expulsion, and loss of medals and other awards. While PEDs can enhance performance, think twice before taking the risk.

Alcohol, of course, is legal, but that also potentially makes it a bigger problem than drugs. The social pressure to "have a few with the guys after a game" is intense, but stars like the NBA's Charles Barkley (who once played a game drunk), Hall of Fame third baseman Wade Boggs (who bragged that he could drink 107 beers in a day) and Green Bay Packers star quarterback Brett Favre (who was also addicted to painkillers) would tell you that excessive drinking can impair judgment and lead to terrible decision making—something that could prove catastrophic for a publicly known athlete with a high-value brand.

As with all things, moderation is the key. Talk to your league, your coach, or someone else you trust about dealing with the temptations of drugs and alcohol. And if you or a teammate has a problem with either, try calling the US Substance Abuse and Mental Health Service Administration Hotline at 800-662-HELP.

ILLEGITIMATE CHILDREN

NBA "Rain Man" Shawn Kemp had at least seven children with six different women, according to *Sports Illustrated*. *SI* also says that Kansas City Chiefs linebacker Derrick Thomas had seven kids with five women. But former NFL running back Travis Henry takes the cake: nine kids with nine different women, according to the *New York Times*. In an example of what can go wrong when you "spread your seeds" so widely, Henry also went to prison for nonpayment of $170,000 in back child support, says *Business Insider*. Meanwhile, the *Atlanta Journal-Constitution* reported that despite earning more than $240 million in the ring, boxing champ Evander Holyfield nearly lost his home because of child support payments close to $500,000 a year.

For the professional athlete, nothing good will come out of an ugly court battle over unpaid child support—or worse, prosecution for nonpayment. The athlete winds up in court in a very public proceeding, looking like a bad guy who wants to stiff his child and dodge his responsibility. He's stuck with the legal fees and a rash of terrible press that would make a publicist nauseous. If he's charged under some state's "deadbeat dad" laws, the penalties could include wage garnishment, negative effects on his immigration status, dings to his credit rating, and in some cases, criminal charges.

As I said earlier, if you can, avoid this trap by being smart in your sexual affairs. Always insist on a pregnancy test and a paternity test. And if you do have a child out of wedlock, step up and take care of your obligations. The public will be a lot more forgiving of an athlete who had a sexual "oops!" than one who runs away from his responsibilities.

SOCIAL MEDIA

Sharing your experiences on social media is fun and doing it well helps you build your following and your online brand. But social media can also be a trap if you share something you shouldn't have, or pop off like QB Drew Brees did after the Black Lives Matter protests last spring. It's easy to forget that social media is a) public, b) global, and c) very shar-able, even if you delete your post or tweet. It's easy to do lasting damage to your reputation in seconds, without even realizing what you've done.

For instance, in 2017 NBA superstar Kevin Durant got busted and embarrassed on Twitter. Apparently, KD had a couple of alias accounts he would switch to when he responded to fans tweeting criticism of his play—except for that one time when he forgot to switch accounts but still wrote like he was just some fan sticking up for Durant. Ouch. That's what they call a "self-own."

Don't let social media trip you up. Use an app like Flipd to lock you out of your social accounts when you're out drinking or in some other situation where you could post something regrettable. Also, make sure there's someone on your personal team who monitors your social feeds and has permission to delete potentially problematic posts and tweets as soon as they appear. And if you're in the middle of a divorce or some other sensitive time in your life, suspend your accounts and stay away.

RUNNING YOUR MOUTH IN THE PRESS

Sometimes, the self-own comes through a foot lodged in the mouth. Back in 1990 MLB outfielder Pete Incaviglia said, "People think we make $3 million and $4 million a year. They don't realize that most of us only make $500,000." Yeah, people making $50,000 a year back then were really feeling sorry for Pete, LOL. Then there was New York Knicks center Patrick Ewing, then president of the NBA Players Association, who said during the 1998 NBA strike, "We might make a lot of money, but we also spend a lot of money."

SMH . . .

In the movie *Bull Durham*, there's a classic scene where Kevin Cost-ner's lifelong minor leaguer Crash Davis is coaching Tim Robbins's soon-to-be big leaguer "Nuke" LaLoosh on how to talk to the media with nothing but empty clichés. When you see how many players cause themselves headaches saying something dumb to a reporter or in front of a microphone, you can see why that scene resonates. Shooting off your mouth in the press can cost you sponsors and even your starting job and damage your brand.

If you're concerned about talking to the press, get some media coaching. If you have a publicist, they should be able to hook you up. If not, many companies offer programs on how to speak to reporters, calm your emotions before an interview, slow down the interview, handle tough questions, and avoid certain subjects.

GUILT BY ASSOCIATION

In other words, hanging with the wrong people can get you into trouble even if you haven't done anything wrong. Imagine you're hosting a party and a woman gets sexually assaulted in one of your spare bedrooms. Who gets sued? You do, because you're the famous one with the deep pockets. Or let's say you're at a strip club with some buddies and get a very suggestive lap dance—but what you don't know is that the date of one of your buddies is filming the dance with her phone and now she wants money from you or she'll send the video to your wife and your church.

When it comes to the company you keep, live by one simple rule:

You are who you hang with.

If some of the people in your life represent an unacceptable risk to your brand, be ruthless about cutting them loose. This is your public image and future earning power we're talking about here, and that's serious business. People with criminal pasts, unsavory friends, drug issues, problems with violence, a habit of popping off on social media—get rid of them. Yes, some will say you've "gone Hollywood." Yes, some will accuse you of being "bougie." Let them. Having lowlifes around makes you vulnerable, and that's easy to fix.

LAWSUITS

You're going to be sued. Accept it. Especially if you live in the United States, if you're (perceived as) rich and famous, you're a target for litigation. So be ready to be sued, possibly by people whom you know, possibly by friends. But also, prepare and plan to reduce the damage:

- Set up multiple LLCs to hold your investments. An LLC can shield your assets against personal litigation.

- Put some assets into irrevocable trusts that protect them from legal judgments.

- Avoid getting into business partnerships, even with friends. When things fall apart, lawsuits tend to fly.

- Never cosign a loan for anything. If someone you care about needs help buying a car, write them a check.

- Make sure you have enough insurance. Your homeowner's policy will cover some liability, but if you're making millions of dollars a year, you should have an umbrella policy with at least five million dollars in coverage. Umbrella coverage is cheap to buy, and it can protect you from wage garnishments and judgments against your assets. Get it.

- Most importantly, get the best possible counsel. When it comes to the issue of contracts, seek the guidance of an attorney. When you're looking at trusts and LLCs, talk to your CFO. When umbrella coverage is on the table, talk to an insurance professional. Always have a good legal team on your side and follow their advice.

IDENTITY THEFT

Remember the story of the NBA star who had his credit card info lifted to the tune of $500,000 in fraudulent charges? That's identity theft, and it's a plague. The thing is, it's preventable with some pretty straightforward actions:

- Again, never, ever give any friends or teammates the usernames and passwords to any of your accounts—not Amazon, not Netflix, not anything. Certainly not your bank or credit cards.

- Freeze your credit reports from Experian, Equifax, and TransUnion. This will prevent anyone from applying for credit in your name. You can always unfreeze them when you want to apply for a loan.

- Have a staffer change your important account passwords on the first day of each month. Use something like LastPass.com to generate random, unguessable passwords.

- Use credit cards that offer fraud protection, like Discover and Capital One Visa cards.

- Never click on suspicious emails or texts, as these can secretly install malware onto your phone or laptop that can steal your personal information. When in doubt, delete it.

- Get or activate a service that tells you when an incoming call to your mobile phone is potential spam. Most cell carriers now offer this feature.

I was going to suggest contracting with a credit monitoring service like LifeLock, but they've come under some criticism of late. However, these services, which monitor your personal information and alert you if anyone tries to use it without your authorization, can be a strong line of defense. Money website The Simple Dollar recommends Identity Guard.

CONTRACTUALLY BANNED ACTIVITIES

Some contracts prohibit athletes from engaging in off-the-field activities that present a high risk of injury. Engaging in such activities could cause the team to void your contract. For example, back in 2005, Cleveland Browns tight end Kellen Winslow Jr. was riding a motorcycle—an activity prohibited in his six-year, $40 million contract—when he flipped and tore his ACL. He was lucky the Browns didn't demand the return of some of the money. Of course, he's now a convicted sex offender, so the money and his knee are probably the least of his worries these days.

Be smart. Stay away from banned activities. Put someone on your team in charge of being the bad guy and enforcing the prohibitions.

WHAT YOU HAVE TO LOSE

Is all this caution and planning and fear overblown? Only if you don't want to keep what you've earned and have a prosperous life after thirty-five. Consider this: there are financial firms that specialize in another type of client who, like professional athletes, come into sudden wealth for which they are unprepared: *lottery winners*.

The comparison is apt. Pro athletes and lottery winners have a lot in common. Both become wealthy relatively quickly and rarely have the background to know what to do with that wealth or how to safeguard it. As a result, both tend to make foolish financial decisions that can lead to bad outcomes.

That's the message I'm trying to send with this chapter. Few people are truly good at making sound financial decisions; they don't have the education, and money is an emotional subject. That's doubly true for pro athletes, who earn more money at a younger age than almost anyone and have no time to become educated about protecting it. As a result, some tend to live like they have nothing to lose—but they do. *You* do. Let me show you all the ways that bad decisions and irresponsible behavior can cost you:

CONSEQUENCE	FINANCIAL LOSS IN DOLLARS
Lost endorsement income	Potentially millions
Child support payments	Hundreds of thousands annually until age eighteen
Divorce settlements	Potentially millions, plus spousal support
Criminal fines	Tens of thousands
IRS penalties	Potentially millions
Lost income due to suspension	Potentially millions
Voiding of your contract	Potentially tens of millions
Legal judgments	Potentially all your assets and property

But none of those grim outcomes is necessary, not with foresight, planning, discipline, and a team that you trust. You can put boundaries in place today that will keep you and your brand safe and sound. Run every social plan beyond a casual dinner with a small group past your business manager or personal assistant and have him or her do a risk analysis on it. If it's too risky, modify the plans. Have someone dedicated to monitoring your social feeds, financial and identity data, press coverage, and the like.

Let your team handle 90 percent of media inquiries and personal requests. Only the legit stuff gets to you; the boneheaded stuff stays off your radar. Give your personal security guard permission to remove you from potentially compromising situations, even over your own objections. Set up limits on your credit and debit cards. Have a driver, even if it's your personal security guy, so you don't have issues with drinking or moving violations. Have professionals install a state-of-the-art home security system, including a full array of security cameras.

Perhaps most importantly of all, make sure you maintain close relationships with those friends and family members who you know you can trust. They are the people who want what's best for you, who will have your back, and who will call you out when you're about to make a bad decision. That's the best security system of all.

OVERTIME

One security measure *not* to take: do not put hidden video cameras in your bedroom to protect you from false sexual harassment or assault allegations. In most states, it's illegal to record hidden camera video in areas where people have a reasonable expectation of privacy—such as bedrooms and bathrooms. You might find yourself slapped with a nasty lawsuit for violating someone's right to privacy.

Technically, if you have visible security cameras in your bedroom and you disclose their presence to a potential sexual partner, that's legal. But it's also problematic. What if the other person consents to the cameras, you have sex, but then the footage leaks to the internet? Do you disclose your "bedroom cams" on your NDA? My advice is to forget the cameras and use your good judgment to figure out who should be in your bedroom.

CHAPTER SIX

How Many Houses Do You Need?

We roll up to the club in a Bentley. All eyes are on us as we stroll toward the door in our Tom Ford suits. We know we're going to get comped at the door. We play for the Orlando Magic and they comp us every time . . . NBA players live a life of fame and full-out fortune. Well-known and recognizable on the street, the average basketball player earns $5.15 million per year. It's no wonder these twentysomethings are all over the club scene, hotels, strip clubs, and anywhere else women congregate. It's a nonstop party.

I played in the NBA for thirteen years, and over those years, I saw extravagances that you would believe a movie director dreamed up, from "makin' it rain" thousands at a time to pouring Moet on naked women. It's all part of an athlete's lifestyle.

—Adonal Foyle, *Winning the Money Game: Lessons Learned From the Financial Fouls of Pro Athletes*

In his book Mr. Foyle goes on to talk about the palatial homes of superstars like LeBron James, who owns a thirty-thousand-square-foot mansion, the luxury vacations, the fleets of cars. You know the drill.

Stories of pro athletes' profligate spending circulate like rumors in high school. They're part of the mythology. But like most myths, they fail to tell the entire story. The rest of the story goes like this: *Wealthy athlete spends like a drunken sailor. Wealthy athlete doesn't have anyone tracking spending and income. Wealthy athlete has no idea where the money is going and winds up spending three or four times what he thought. Wealthy athlete wakes up one day broke and deeply in debt.*

It's a sadly common horror story:

- In 2010, quarterback Vince Young signed a $25 million contract with the Tennessee Titans and very nearly went on to win the Super Bowl. By 2014 he had declared bankruptcy. Why? Well, how about well-documented spending habits like buying $600 shots of cognac and routinely spending $5,000 at the Cheesecake Factory? (The *Cheesecake Factory*, Vince? Come on . . .)

- St. Louis Cardinals and San Francisco Giants slugger Jack Clark filed for bankruptcy not once but twice. The first filing, in 1992, came about in part because Clark was unable to maintain the payments on his *eighteen* luxury automobiles.

- Boxing legend Evander Holyfield banked more than $310 million in his career, so in 2019 why was he living in a two-bedroom apartment? Because, among other things, he bought a 109-room Atlanta mansion that he was eventually evicted from after falling $14 million behind in mortgage payments. Failed marriages and failed business ventures did the rest of the damage.

I could go on, and on, and on, but I won't. The outrageous spending habits of top pro athletes are legendary and have become the standard by which an athlete's success is often measured. But there's a big difference when guys like Tom Brady and Michael Jordan spend $25 million or more to buy and trick out their Gulfstream private jets. Those guys are legends, industries all to themselves, and they can afford those extravagances. But they're the .0001 percent of pro athletes who can. The rest, which almost certainly includes you, have to be far more careful with their money. The problem with the very visible big spenders is that they create an expectation: *this is how athletes live, and if you're not living this way, you're a loser.*

Speaking in the *Pittsburgh Post-Gazette* in 2017, Matt Helfrich, president of Waldron Private Wealth, a financial firm that works with athletes and celebrities, said that pro athletes who wind up burning through millions get tripped up by a sense of entitlement that makes them believe that owning multiple homes, investing in bars and restaurants, and even owning a private jet are simply required.

"During their careers, athletes and entertainers are used to private flying," Helfrich said in the *Post-Gazette* story. "They want to carry over that lifestyle after their career is over. But they don't understand the costs associated with it or the waste that can be incurred by not structuring the costs properly. Also, they buy homes for themselves, vacation homes, and homes for their friends and family members. All of the homes have carrying costs with them. There are taxes, maintenance, landscaping, cable, and staffs. That's even before considering if they paid too much."

TEPPER TIP

Inflation

You might hear people talk about inflation—the decline in money's purchasing power due to a small but steady increase in prices over time—but it doesn't register. That's because inflation right now is historically low. However, over time inflation reduces the buying power of your money. For example, let's say you've invested wisely and have $15.5 million in assets. Assuming a 2.5 percent annual inflation rate (because things get more expensive every year), in twenty years that $15.5 million will have the same buying power as $9.4 million today. To put it simply, your money loses value over time. That's why it's not a good idea to have too much of your money in cash accounts, where it might earn less than 1 percent. Your investments must earn enough to outpace inflation or you're actually losing purchasing power every year.

ASSETS VERSUS LIABILITIES

Imagine you're a young athlete who just signed a contract with a team worth $100 million. You're euphoric. This is the big payoff you've been working toward all your life. Finally, you can take care of your parents, take care of your wife and kids, and live the dream life you've always wanted. You are most definitely *not* thinking about the fact that taxes, commissions, and other expenses will give your gross income a 50 percent haircut before it ever reaches your bank account. You're not thinking about interest rates on credit cards, the total cost of ownership of a new house or new car, or anything else like that. Your Board of Directors *would* be thinking about those matters, but you don't have one.

As soon as you start getting those big checks, you go on a buying spree: a Benz for your commute, an Escalade for going out with your boys, and a twenty-thousand-square-foot mini-mansion for you, your wife, and your two children. You pay off your mother and father's mortgage, spend $250,000 on furnishings for your new place, hire domestic staff, host a huge party to celebrate, and live happily ever after. Right?

Not so much. Because you're not Tom Brady or Michael Jordan, with their monster brands and business ventures that will keep making them millions long after their careers have ended. Your money is finite, but it doesn't *feel* that way. So you don't negotiate on price or shop for deals, because you don't *have* to. You invest in risky start-up businesses—instead of "boring" instruments like mutual funds and stocks—because it's an adrenaline rush.

As a result, after a year or two, you're saddled with *massive* debt and very little liquidity (cash or assets that can easily be converted into cash). You're carrying a $25,000 monthly mortgage payment, $50,000 combined balances on multiple credit cards, big nuts for car payments, cell phone plans, travel, and regular expenses like paying your personal staff. Because of this, you have very few long-term investments and virtually no savings. You tell yourself everything is okay because you're still playing and there's another nine-figure contract in your future, but what if there isn't? What if you get hurt or just get cut? What if your spouse files for divorce or you're the defendant in a huge lawsuit?

Consider JJ Watt, NFL defensive end and a three-time Defensive Player of the Year who was released by the Houston Texans. Watt was still a top-tier defensive player when healthy, but he'd struggled to stay on the field. With $17.5 million due on his contract in 2021 and the Texans over the salary cap, unloading his salary was more valuable to the team than his services. Bottom line, nobody's indispensable, and stuff happens.

Athletes who find themselves in dire financial straits often misunderstand the definition of wealth. In the world of professional financial management, when we talk about a client's overall financial standing, we frequently speak in terms of his *net worth*. Net worth has nothing to do with your *income*, the amount of money you have coming in through salary, bonuses, endorsements, or prize purses. That's the metric that so many athletes look at because it's pleasurable to look at the big numbers coming into your bank account through direct deposit. But as the old saying goes, it's not how much you make, it's how much you keep. That's why in finance we look at net worth, which is based on a very simple calculation:

Assets – Liabilities = Net Worth

Investopedia defines an asset as a resource with economic value, which is just right. Assets fall into different categories—current, fixed, financial, intangible—but for our purposes, I'm going to keep this simple. For professional athletes, assets will usually fall into a few classes:

- Fixed assets such as real estate
- Current assets like cash and the future value of a contract
- Financial assets like stocks, bonds, and equity investments in businesses

The key to our conversation is understanding the other side of the equation, *liability*. A liability is an amount of money that you are obligated to pay: a mortgage debt, a car loan, child support payments, a student loan, and so on. When you know your assets and your liabilities, figuring out your net worth is easy:

Net Worth = What You Own – What You Owe

Suppose you're a professional athlete who owns the following assets:

ASSET	MARKET VALUE
Primary residence	$4.5 million
Vacation home	$1.2 million
Main car	$125,000
Second car	$75,000
30 percent equity in small business	$500,000
Cash savings	$25,000

Just looking at your assets, you're worth **$6.225 million**. Not bad. Well, not so fast. Because now you have to consider your liabilities, which include not only what you owe on your possessions but also any other debts:

DEBT	AMOUNT
Mortgage on primary residence	$3.6 million
Mortgage on vacation home	$850,000
Balance on car loan #1	$86,000
Balance on car loan #2	$60,000
Total credit card balances	$47,000
Federal back taxes owed	$115,000

Your liabilities add up to **$4,758,000.** But that's not the end of it. That $500,000 you invested in your former college roommate's "software" company? It's probably lost because the company is close to going under. That drops the value of your assets to $5.725 million, which means your "true" net worth is:

$$\$5,725,000 - 4,758,000 = \$967,000$$

LIABILITY = VULNERABILITY

Now, I've oversimplified this in the extreme to avoid making your eyes glaze over; in my work, computing a client's true net worth is far more complex and involves many more variables. But I hope I've made my point with this stripped-down example. When you consider what you owe, your net worth is probably much, much less than you think.

But the critical part of net worth that I want you to remember and make part of your financial thinking is this:

Liability equals vulnerability.

"Talking about net worth doesn't really resonate with athletes," says Lauryn Williams, an American Olympic sprinter and bobsledder who won multiple medals before becoming a CFP® and working with fellow Olympians. "So I don't really talk net worth so much as I ask, 'Where are you vulnerable? Where are you vulnerable on the field if you don't do your training appropriately? Where are you vulnerable off the field?'"

For athletes who seem unstoppable, it's easy to become complacent. But the value of your assets is often as volatile as your career path. The real estate market goes up and down, as does the stock market. So your assets can become more valuable but also less valuable. Meanwhile, unless you pay it off, your debt remains a predictable amount; your mortgage balance doesn't shrink in sympathy because the market value of your house drops by 20 percent. Some debt, such as credit card debt, can actually increase if you don't make sufficient payments to keep the balance moving downward—not to mention ruining your credit score.

Finally, there's the income volatility that's a fact of life for 95 percent of pro athletes. When you have a serious injury, a run of bad luck, or are a birthday away from being an ex-athlete, you're also potentially a whisper away from financial catastrophe if you're carrying a great deal of debt. That's vulnerability.

Again, as long as everything is going well in your life and the money is flowing from your salary, prize purses, or shoe deals, this may not seem like such a big deal. But how often does life go smoothly for very long? Shit happens. Marriages fall apart. Businesses fail. Stock markets crater. You get slapped with a lawsuit. You blow out your elbow. You get cut. Liability equals vulnerability because it kills your resilience when things are not so good.

That's how multimillionaires like Evander Holyfield wind up losing everything. When you're overspending and carrying enough debt to sink a Nimitz-class aircraft carrier, things can go bad very quickly. When creditors demand payment or a court renders a financial judgment and you don't have the cash to pay, you can end up filing bankruptcy or selling your assets for a fraction of what they're worth, leaving you with nothing in the end. That's a terrible coda to a career you worked hard for and that you hoped would at least leave you comfortable going into the future.

THE "COMFORT AND PEACE" STANDARD

The main reason some highly paid pro athletes wind up poor is not that they make bad investments or are victims of fraud. It's that they don't act as though their career earnings have to last the rest of their lives. They spend foolishly. They overconsume to fuel their lifestyles. They do that because they think about spending in the wrong way. I don't want to see that happen to you, so I'm going to teach you the correct way to think about spending.

When we think about athlete financial success stories, we should be looking at guys like Washington Redskins defensive end Ryan Kerrigan, former NBA Rookie of the Year Michael Carter-Williams, and Detroit Tigers pitcher Daniel Norris. Kerrigan is notoriously frugal. Even after signing a five-year, $57.5-million contract in 2015, he didn't splurge on a mansion. He got an apartment with a childhood friend, Andrew Walker. And when Kerrigan isn't cooking for himself at home, his big food expenditure is Chipotle. I feel you, Ryan. Those burrito bowls are epic. As for Carter-Williams, when he signed a $10 million rookie contract in 2013 with the Philadelphia 76ers, his parents immediately put his first year's salary—$4.5 million minus income taxes—into a trust fund that he couldn't touch for three years. Carter-Williams lived off his endorsement income. It proved to be a smart move, too, as his career (and income) has been on a downward slide ever since that magical debut season.

But the most extreme is Norris. When the Tigers drafted him in June of 2011, they paid him a $2 million bonus. With what he received after taxes, he bought a 1978 Volkswagen Westfalia camper van and invested the remainder, more than $1 million, in the stock market. Norris gave himself an $800 monthly stipend and—get this—lived in the van. The rest of the money grew. He's continued to live his minimalist lifestyle through thyroid cancer in 2015 and even after signing several seven-figure deals. He also had the good fortune to invest near the beginning of one of the longest bull markets in history. So while his finances are private, let's say Norris invested that $1 million solely in the S&P 500 beginning in July 2011. If he didn't add or withdraw funds, by March 2021, he would have enjoyed an annualized rate of return (including dividends) of 13.9 percent. That initial $1 million would have become about $3.5 million.

Now, it's understandable that you would want to splurge a little after making a big payday, especially if you grew up without a lot of money. You want to show off your success and enjoy a little luxury, take care of your family, show some love to your friends. Cool. But it's important to enjoy your money in a way that doesn't jeopardize your future.

Here's where many athletes (and nonathletes) go off the rails: they spend according to what I call the Affordability Standard. Meaning, when they are looking to buy something, the ceiling for what they'll spend is what they can afford. If you're house hunting, and you make enough to afford a $12,000 monthly mortgage payment (before real estate taxes), that will buy you a house worth around $2.5 million. So that's what you buy. If you're looking for a car and your income will cover the $300,000 cost of a Mercedes Maybach GLS class, that's what you buy. You spend right up to the limit of what you can afford for everything.

The trouble with that, of course, is that word again—vulnerability. If you're constantly maxed out, you have no financial flexibility for dealing with the inevitable ugly surprises of life, like car repairs, home repairs, and medical bills. You're spending 100 percent of your net income, or more. How does someone spend more than 100 percent? Easy. Debt. When you're burning through every penny you take home for your mortgage, car loans, utilities, and living expenses and an unexpected bill comes in, you're putting that sucker on your Amex. That adds up fast, and before you know it, you've got $25,000 in credit card debt at 18 percent interest.

I want you to start governing your shopping and other financial decisions according to the Comfort and Peace Standard. That means that instead of spending as much as you can afford, you spend as much as you feel comfortable spending—an amount that gives you peace of mind because you know you're not overextended. You have money available to cover emergencies, surprises, and unexpected costs.

Suppose you're house hunting using this standard. You walk through the $2.5 million house with its 7,200 square feet, six bedrooms, four-car garage, and home theater. But it's just you and your fiancée, so why do you need that much house? You don't. You're much more comfortable buying a still very nice $500,000 house with four bedrooms, a great kitchen, and a pool for entertaining. When you shop for a car, you test drive the Lambo Aventador because you've always wanted to, but you don't like the $400,000 price tag. You and your girl still want a fun sports car, so you pay $100,000 cash for a Porsche. Now you have a manageable mortgage payment and no car loan.

This way of thinking about your spending ties into something I call the **Wealth Standard**. It's a way of thinking about money and your lifestyle that will free you of the need to keep up with your teammates and burn cash on luxuries you don't need. The Wealth Standard says that feeling wealthy or being seen as wealthy doesn't matter. You want to *be* wealthy, and being wealthy means having a comfortable lifestyle, being able to buy and enjoy the things and experiences you want within reason, having peace of mind because you're not overextended, carrying little or no debt, having emergency funds saved, and having a plan for the future.

When you have all that, you're wealthy. Superficial wealth isn't wealth at all if it means you're deep in debt, burdened with bad investments, and always on the brink of bankruptcy because you've spent everything you make. Too many athletes ruin their futures because they get caught up in appearing like players who can make it rain. Don't fall into that trap. It's a lot more fun to be wealthy for life than to live extravagantly for a few years.

KNOW THE SCORE

When you sign your first big contract or get your first signing bonus, immediately start saving an emergency fund. You'll put at least 30 percent of your net income in zero-risk instruments like certificates of deposit (CDs) until you have saved enough to cover all your expenses for one year. This is your emergency cash, the money you could use to cover all your expenses and pay all your debt payments if you were injured or suffered some other catastrophe. Remember the formula I introduced in Chapter Three? Suppose your predictable annual living expenses (food, gas, school tuition, etc.) plus debt service (mortgage, credit card payments, etc.) come to about $250,000 a year. After taxes and commissions, your career nets you about $75,000 a month. Have your CFO set up an automatic transfer that puts $22,500 of that $75,000 into your emergency account. In twelve months, you'll have more than $250,000 saved. Now, forget it's there and stop the automatic transfer so you can invest everything else you earn.

THE OUTGO

A lot of this just requires common sense and thinking ahead, plus a dedication to living according to that Wealth Standard. Solomon Wilcots explains:

I needed a whole other level of understanding when it came to finances when I came out of college. I talked to my agent and I said, "I need you to help me with these things, and I'm going to need this well beyond my playing career." He and I would meet every year after the season was over, and we'd go over my finances. This was just making sure I was smart, and we'd work out a budget for the year. So I have always lived on a budget, and never lived a free-spending life. I've never known what that was like.

I remember even restructuring my pay. Most NFL players are paid one sixteenth or one seventeenth of their salary for every week, so if you're getting paid one million dollars, after every game, you get one seventeenth of a million dollars. When the season's over, you've gotten your whole salary. I was like, "No, I don't want to do that. I want to be paid biweekly all year around." The team was all, "Why does he do that?" Well, I wouldn't know what to do with a check that big, and I wanted help budgeting my money and spreading it out, just like everyday people who get paid on a biweekly basis or a monthly basis. I also didn't want to go the whole off-season without getting paid. That's what happens to some guys: they end up spending a lot of their salary during the season and then they've got nothing to get them to the next season.

That's how do to this right. That's controlling your income and enforcing discipline on yourself, which is especially important when you're young. On the other extreme, you could buy tigers. *Don't buy tigers.* Let's call that an ironclad rule. Tigers bite. They smell. Joe "Tiger King" Exotic owned tigers, and he's in prison. Mike Tyson bought three Bengal tigers as pets and over one year, they cost him more than $530,000. Then again, he also spent $2.2 million on a solid gold bathtub for his wife, which makes the three tigers look like a bargain.

You should have fun with your money; that's what it's for, in part! But know where your money is going, and prioritize what you do with it. Have a plan. Spending blindly is a trap that can ruin you. It's not just your income that matters, it's your "outgo," the money you waste daily without even realizing it, that adds up.

So let's take a look at that spending. Let's look at the typical expenses of a professional athlete of average wealth living a moderately plush lifestyle in a popular city, Los Angeles. Let's look at how it all adds up.

EVERYDAY EXPENSES

EXPENSE CATEGORY	AVERAGE COST/MONTH	NOTES
First Home	$2.5 million price	5 bed, 5 bath, 4,000 sq. ft.
Mortgage	$10,000	$2 million loan, 30 yrs.
Property Taxes	$1,562	
Insurance	$600	
Upkeep	$850	
Staff	$4,800	Housekeeping, landscaping

Vacation Home	$1.5 million price	Location: Palm Springs
Mortgage	$7,200	$1.2 million loan, 30 yrs.
Property Taxes	$1,050	
Insurance	$450	
Upkeep	$500	
Staff	$4,800	Housekeeping, land-scaping

Primary Car (BMW 740i)	$100,000	
Loan Payment	$1,441	$80,000 loan, 5 yrs.
Maintenance	$90	
Insurance	$167	

Second Car (Range Rover)	$120,000	
Loan Payment	$1,802	$100,000 loan, 5 yrs.

Maintenance	$100	
Insurance	$180	

Fun Car (Porsche Boxster)	$80,000	
Loan Payment	$1,153	$64,000 loan, 5 yrs.
Maintenance	$110	
Insurance	$180	

Boat (Beneteau Monte Carlo 52)	$1.3 million	
Loan Payment	$7,650	$1 million loan, 15 yrs.
Maintenance	$250	
Insurance	$100	
Slip Fees	$1,300	

Personal Services	
Attorney	$350/hour, estimate 6 hours/month = $2,100
CPA	$200/hour, estimate 10 hours/month = $2,000
Personal Security	$4,000
Valet	$6,000
Trainer	12 sessions/month @ $100/session = $1,200
Chef	$2,000
Personal Asst.	$2,500

Possessions	
Clothing	$1,000
Jewelry & Watches	$1,000

Electronics	$1,000	
Fitness & Athletic Gear	$1,000	
Toys	$1,000	

Miscellaneous		
Private School Tuition	$3,000	Assuming 2 kids
Credit Card Payments	$3,000	Assuming a $20,000 balance
Life Insurance	$50	$1 million policy
Umbrella Insurance	$50	$5 million policy

TOTAL MONTHLY EXPENSES	$77,235

That's about $925,000 a year, and that's without considering costs like groceries, utilities, dining out, entertainment, and travel, which will definitely come into play. Factor in those additional costs and you could easily be looking at $1.2 million a year just in basic living expenses. Let's say you're making $5 million a year in salary from your team. You're only netting $2.5 million of that because of taxes and commissions, and you're burning 50 percent of your take-home income on monthly lifestyle expenses. You're also carrying millions in debt, and that might not seem like a big deal when you're playing. But when you retire and the income faucet turns off but those debts are still there, it is a *very* big deal.

(In addition, in this scenario, you've dropped about $1.1 million in down payments on your houses, cars, and boat. So even though those aren't recurring expenses, that money is spent.)

If you're also paying for a house for your parents, giving your friends cash or covering their bills, or sinking money into their business ventures, your outgo is going to rise even more. Suddenly, you're burning $1.5 million a year and have only $1 million for priorities like savings, investments, and an emergency fund, which everyone should have.

You've also left yourself vulnerable to reversals like getting injured, being cut from your team, being named in a lawsuit, being hit with child support, or being the subject of a social media scandal that costs you endorsements.

The good news is, a lot of this wasteful monthly spending is unnecessary. There are commonsense ways to save money, prevent waste, and dial back your outgo without sacrificing any parts of the lifestyle you enjoy. In fact, you'll probably enjoy your life more because you'll have greater peace of mind.

TIME-OUT

The problem with noncash forms of payment like credit cards or Apple Pay is that when you don't see your money dwindling, you're less aware of what you're spending. So, while I don't recommend that you carry a fat wad of cash around at all times because it can mark you as a target for thieves and unscrupulous people, try to get in the habit of using cash for your daily spending instead of plastic or apps as often as possible. Doing so makes your regular spending feel more real, which in turn makes it easier to curb wasteful spending on things like expensive coffee, valet parking, and fast food—costs that can add up fast.

BUDGET YOURSELF

One of the most important steps you can take in ensuring your future financial security is getting control over your monthly spending. The best way to do that, and a mandatory one in my opinion, is to put yourself on a budget. "We always start with a budget," says Lauryn Williams. "The most important thing is having a strong foundation so [athletes] understand where money is coming in, where it's going, and how to work within the parameters of what's reasonable so that they can stabilize their income and then to start to create wealth."

Sit down with your CFO and business manager, and go through all the ways you spend money every month, dividing them into the following classifications:

- **Debts and Commitments.** These are things like loan and tax payments that you are required to make. Your COO or CFO should arrange to have these made electronically each month.

- **Nondiscretionary Costs.** These are expenses you have committed to as part of your lifestyle: utilities, internet, insurance premiums, school tuition, salaries for your staff, payroll taxes for staff, and so on. Your team should also arrange to have these all paid electronically, but not automatically. For safety, someone should approve these expenses each month.

- **Discretionary Spending.** This is your optional spending on things like food, dining out, clothing, gifts, travel, gasoline, and so on. This is a major source of waste, so this is where a budget will be most helpful.

- **Predictable Surprises.** Sounds contradictory, but this category refers to expenses that you can't predict but you know are inevitable, like car repairs, home repairs, and medical bills. These expenses are best covered by a reserve of cash you have in a bank account somewhere. Remember the emergency fund we talked about earlier?

   The category of expenses that most needs managing is discretionary spending. Having a budget in this area can help you be mindful of what you're spending and also help you avoid dropping a few thousand dollars while you're at dinner with friends, tipping a cute server $1,000, or blowing $7,650 on a handmade Hermès maplewood trash can, which is a thing. After you've gone through your expenses in the other three categories, dig into what a reasonable monthly budget might look like.

The best way to do this is to go back six months and look at all your discretionary spending. Then, mercilessly divide it into three groups:

- **Group 1: Essentials.** Meals, groceries, utilities, coffee, gasoline, postage, parking, tolls, basic stuff you need to live day-to-day. Add it all up and come up with a monthly average.

- **Group 2: Optionals.** Movie tickets, concert tickets, Netflix, Grubhub, Uber, casino spending, Amazon purchases, room service, nonbusiness travel. Total it up, get your monthly average, and cut it in half.

- **Group 3: Dumb Stuff.** Buying tigers, buying a seventh Rolex, throwing a $10,000 party for strangers, huge tips, bottle service in excess of your self-imposed cap. This stuff is *gone*. You don't need it.

Add your group 1 number and group 2 number (remember, you're cutting this total in half), then add another 20 percent for surprises and small luxuries, and you have your monthly budget. So if you'd been spending $5,000 a month on essentials, $6,000 a month on optionals, and $5,000 a month on dumb stuff, your new monthly budget is:

$$(\$5,000 + \$3,000) \times 120\% = \$9,600$$

That's your number, and you have to stick to it. No going over. No splurging. No calling your CPA at home at 1:45 a.m. because it's two days until your budget resets and you had your heart set on treating the table to one more bottle of Don Julio Real. The best way to manage this—at least in the beginning, when you're trying to break bad habits and put in place smart spending patterns—is to use a prepaid debit card when you go out.

These cards, issued by companies like Green Dot and others in the Visa Clear Prepaid program, let you preload a card with a set amount, and when that money's gone, it's gone. That keeps you from spending mindlessly because you know if you do, you might run out of money on the twenty-seventh of the month and spend the next four days stuck at home or borrowing from teammates and feeling like an idiot.

A few tips about prepaid debit cards. First, they sometimes come with a lot of fees, so have your CFO or CPA shop around for the best deal. Second, make this foolproof by only letting your COO (your business manager) recharge the card with money. It's not a curb on your spending if you can violate it on a whim. Third, cancel your other cards or lock them in your home safe. If you don't have them when you go out, you can't use them. Finally, make sure you can't make impulse online purchases by deleting other card information from sites like Amazon and iTunes.

Keep in mind, I'm not trying to deny you the use of your money. You can still use your credit cards and all your resources. Budgeting and using a prepaid debit card is all about reducing your *impulse and unconscious purchases*—the daily latte, the $1,200 dinner, and so on. When you're specifically going shopping for a new suit, take your Amex and get it done. Just don't buy a $10,000 ATV on the way home.

TEPPER TIP

Liquid versus Illiquid Investments

From time to time, you probably hear financial types talking about "liquidity." What is it? Liquidity measures how easy it is to convert an asset into cash without affecting its price. Obviously, cash is the most liquid investment because you don't have to convert it. Stocks are relatively liquid because you can sell them easily, while real estate is more "illiquid," meaning it's harder to turn into cash, in part because it can take a long time to sell.

Here's a good rule to follow about liquid investments versus illiquid investments. Suppose you have a total net worth of $5 million (excluding real estate and cars). No more than 20 percent of that $5 million should be in illiquid investments like businesses, private equity, or franchises. The other 80 percent should be in liquid investments like stocks and mutual funds. This ensures that you can access your money quickly when you need it.

BE A PROFESSIONAL CHEAPSKATE

Green Bay Packers quarterback Aaron Rodgers has made more than $200 million in his career from salary alone, making him one of the highest paid football players in the country. But he lives in a modest suburban house, cuts his own grass, and shops at local supermarkets. Matt Bonner, who had a thirteen-year career in the NBA, mostly with the San Antonio Spurs, became infamous for taking public transportation in some cities and wearing his shoes until they literally fell apart. Former Indianapolis Colts QB Andrew Luck used a flip phone because he didn't want to shell out for a smartphone. NBA superstar Carmelo Anthony clips coupons at the grocery store. He told CheatSheet.com, "I go to the supermarket, make sure I get the newspaper and tear the coupons out, save a dollar or two."

You don't hear much about professional athletes who are also bargain hunters. We tend to hear about the guys who set a few million bucks on fire buying ridiculous houses, fleets of cars, and private aircraft. But the cheapskate athletes are the smart ones because they're living according to the Wealth Standard. They know their careers could end at any time and will end one day, so they don't waste a dime. They would rather live simply, save their money, and have the freedom to live any kind of life they want after their careers are over. Sounds pretty appealing, doesn't it?

This is where you should rely on your financial team because they can help you avoid big financial blunders. "You can make some really expensive mistakes that you don't see in the short term," says Lauryn Williams. "That's why it's important to have wise counsel. You might hear an athlete say, 'I bought a house that was way too big, but you know, I was approved for it.' There were no red flags on his credit, but now he's overcommitted. I would have said, 'This is not sustainable over thirty years in light of your other goals because you're not going to be earning like this forever.'"

There are probably some areas in which you're not willing to compromise on cost. I respect that; I believe that you get what you pay for. But there's no reason any athlete should overpay when you can get comparable quality for much less, and there's no call for getting ripped off. It's time to start thinking like a professional cheapskate—letting the hunt for the best bargain flood you with as much adrenaline as competition. Pick one or two areas where you won't compromise on price—for example, spending a lot on top-quality food and training equipment makes sense for someone whose living depends on a healthy body (I have a personal preference for Rogue fitness gear, which is higher quality and priced accordingly)—and become a ferocious bargain hunter everywhere else. Here are a few examples of how you can save:

- **Real Estate.** Do you really need more than one house? That's why services like Airbnb and Vrbo exist. Rent an awesome retreat when you want to go on vacation and save yourself the carrying costs. Buy as much house as you need for your family to be comfortable. You probably don't need a thirty-thousand-square-foot mansion for a family of four. Realtor.com suggests asking these questions when you're trying to decide how much house you need:

  » Are you planning on living there for a long time?
  » What will your income look like in five or ten years? This is even more important for athletes, who face that end-of-career earnings cliff.

» What are your priorities? Parties? Cooking? Hosting overnight guests?

» How much extra space does everyone need for things like work, schoolwork, working out, and so on?

Huge houses often end up with lots of unused rooms and become anchors around their owners' necks. Find a house that feels comfortable but not extravagant. You know what feels extravagant? Having lots of money in the bank.

TEPPER TIP

What to Spend on Real Estate

Here's a simple guideline for how much you should spend on real estate. If you have a guaranteed contract, take the total guaranteed value of that contract. So, if you signed a $40 million contract with your team, but $20 million of it is guaranteed, $20 million is the number you use. Now, the total value of your real estate purchases should not exceed 10 percent of that guaranteed number. So if you have $20 million guaranteed, you should spend no more than $2 million on your primary residence, a vacation home, whatever (5 percent would be even better, by the way). That applies whether you pay cash or finance.

Speaking of which, should you pay cash for real estate or take on debt? The general rule is that if you're buying a depreciating asset (something that loses value over time) like a car, pay cash if you can, or lease them so you're only paying for the depreciation. If you're buying assets with the potential for appreciation (real estate or a business), it can make sense to use leverage and get financing. And with interest rates as ridiculously low as they are now, it makes even more sense.

- **Vehicles.** You probably only need two cars: a daily "get the kids to school" car and a weekend "fun" car. The trick is to avoid overpaying, and that's easy if you follow one rule: *never buy a new second car again.* I'm okay with you leasing your primary vehicle new. But opt for your second car used. Why? Miles are low. You can get a three- or four-year-old vehicle with fewer than ten thousand miles on it. Plus, cars are so well-made today that even a car that's three or four years old will be reliable, with all the bells and whistles you want, but will cost less to buy and insure.

  What to spend? The total value of all your vehicles should not exceed 2 percent of your guaranteed money. If you take 2 percent of the $20 million from the real estate example above, that's $400,000. Honestly, if you can't get two great vehicles for half that amount, you're not looking very hard. Try Carvana.com, TrueCar.com, and CarGurus.com to find the best deals. (By the way, if you're not in a guaranteed contract situation, use 10 percent of your net annual income as your spending cap for vehicles.)

- **Boats.** This one is simple: *don't buy a boat.* The saying "a boat is a hole in the water where you pour money" is a saying for a reason. Boats depreciate (lose value) faster than cars do and cost a fortune to keep up. If you want a boat for a party, charter one and hire a professional skipper.

- **Aircraft.** Of all the dumb ways athletes waste money, buying a private plane is the dumbest. There is simply no reason to own one. If you're running a far-flung business empire and need to get around without airport hassles, hire a private jet as needed through NetJets, Flexjet, JetSmarter, or Wheels Up. Or just fly commercial and upgrade to first class when you check in.

  Ian Wild, a former NFL and CFL player who's now a CFP® working as a wealth manager, had to resist this temptation when he was playing. "When I was with the Steelers, James Harrison and Antonio

Brown were my locker mates, and during minicamp they would rent private jets and go to Lakers basketball games or different stuff," he says. "And they'd ask me if I wanted to come, and we would all split the cost of the jet. A couple of other guys would go and they'd have to write a check for about thirty-two hundred bucks after the weekend. It was hard for me to turn that down because sure, I want to go party with Antonio Brown, but I was on the practice squad. I was making a thousand bucks a week. I couldn't afford a thirty-two-hundred-dollar weekend. A lot of stuff like that happens."

Hey, at least Ian's teammates were renting jets, not buying them! That's a silver lining.

- **Professional Staff.** Don't hire a bunch of people to service your needs so you can have bragging rights. Instead of paying salaries, benefits, and payroll taxes, use apps like Tidy to hire housekeepers, Zeel to book a massage, and Freshly to order chef-prepared healthy meals delivered right to your door.

- **Home Security.** If you live unostentatiously, skip the expensive home security system and install a DIY system from a provider like SimpliSafe or Ring.

Finally, when you're having your budget summit meeting with your CFO and CPA, make a list called "Negotiables." Your business manager or CFO should be actively shopping for better deals for you on these things: credit cards, loans, cable channels, internet service, hotels, personal services, subscriptions, and the like. Don't sacrifice on quality too much, but save where you can. Remember, rich people stay rich because they spend wisely. For instance, Warren Buffett's favorite steakhouse in Omaha, Gorat's, lists a twenty-two-ounce Omaha T-Bone at $41. That's nothing compared to what "high end" restaurants charge.

You can learn more of these basics, tips, and guidelines for your entire financial life in my Financial Literacy for Athletes video series. Kick back, put your feet up, and get the inside scoop on real estate, leverage, and a lot more in easy-to-understand videos mostly less than five minutes long. Go to WealthLit101.com to sign up.

OVERTIME

One of the best pieces of financial advice I've ever heard directed at pro athletes is this: *Compete against your opponent, not against the guy in the next locker.* Some athletes get so caught up in "living the life" that they feel that if one of their teammates springs for a $10,000 watch, they have to buy a $12,000 one just to show him up. It's the "he who dies with the most toys wins" theory, and that's just wrong. The athletes who obsess over toys and public shows of wealth are the same athletes who wind up declaring bankruptcy.

It's also difficult to live a luxurious life for a few years on a star athlete's salary, only to have your standard of living suddenly drop dramatically after retirement and for the rest of your life. It's much easier to start living a comfortable but sustainable lifestyle *now*. Remember, your goal is peace of mind, happiness, security, and freedom for the future. If you have those things, who cares what the guy in the next locker drives?

CHAPTER SEVEN

MONEY AND INVESTING

When NBA great Kobe Bryant died tragically in a helicopter crash, people rightly memorialized him for a ton of achievements. One that got no attention was the fact that Kobe was one hell of a smart investor. He and partner Jeff Stibel founded a $100 million venture capital fund (a pool of money that makes ground-floor investments in young and start-up businesses) called Bryant Stibel. Bryant also earned praise for a $6 million investment in the sports drink company Body Armor in 2014, a stake that by the spring of 2018 had grown 3,200 percent. Not bad.

Kobe Bryant is far from the only example of a professional athlete who has made smart investment decisions. The most famous might be fellow Los Angeles Lakers great Magic Johnson, who was one of the first big-name NBA stars to take a risk on investing in inner-city areas that no regular bank or VC firm would touch—famously opening Starbucks locations in South Central Los Angeles. Magic Johnson Enterprises, the investment conglomerate Johnson founded in 1987, owns businesses in such sectors as entertainment, education, real estate, life insurance, retail stores, food, and facilities management and runs the Yucaipa Johnson Corporate Initiatives Growth Fund, which focuses on investing in companies working in underserved minority markets. The company has a net worth of at least $1 billion.

Talk about timing. Another NBA player, Andre Iguodala, didn't know much about investing when he left the Golden State Warriors, so he opened an E*TRADE brokerage account to learn about the market. He's a fast learner, because since then he's invested in Zoom (whose stock at the time of this writing had quadrupled in value since April 1, 2020, due to coronavirus-related lockdowns), Derek Jeter–owned athlete communications platform The Players' Tribune, and mattress behemoth Casper, among many others. There must be something in the water in Oakland, because former Golden State Warrior Kevin Durant (Postmates, scooter company Lime) and current Warrior Steph Curry (VC investments including SnapTravel) have also been killing it.

Those are the winners. There have also been many losers. Curt Schilling was a stud pitcher for the Boston Red Sox and Arizona Diamondbacks, but that success didn't translate to finance. He launched his own video game company, 38 Studios, in 2006, but the company managed to release only one game and eventually filed for chapter 7 bankruptcy, taking $50 million of Schilling's personal assets with it. That's called *concentration risk*. Nobody hits every investment out of the park, so by spreading your money around in different investments, you lower your risk and increase your chance of success. Unfortunately for Curt, he failed to diversify.

Former New York Jets Pro Bowl quarterback Mark Brunell made more than $50 million in his career but wound up bankrupt in 2001 after a series of unwise financial decisions. First, he and some teammates borrowed to build Florida condos, but when the real estate market collapsed, Brunell tried to make good on the loans with his own money. He also lost $9 million investing in Whataburger franchises. And former Washington Redskins and Denver Broncos running back Clinton Portis wound up filing for bankruptcy as well after losing more than $5 million, much of it on an investment in an Alabama casino. I could go on and on, but it would be too depressing.

EXPERT PARTNERS

Have you picked up on the biggest difference between the winners and losers in those stories? The winners worked with experienced, expert financial and business partners. The losers either tried to DIY their investments or got bilked by unscrupulous advisors. Kobe, Magic, Iguodala—they all partnered with professionals who came from the worlds of venture capital and private equity investing. They had the assets and the public brands, but they knew they needed to work with people who were superstars in the world of term sheets, bridge loans, and equity rounds. Schilling launched his own game company because he was a video game enthusiast. Brunell's real estate partners were his teammates. The guys who got Portis to invest in the casino were financial advisors who only managed publicly traded investments, not business investment specialists with an eye for private deals.

The message here is simple:

Being an athlete, even a very smart or wealthy athlete, does not make you a financial, business, or investment expert.

Kobe Bryant was an extremely intelligent man. So is Magic Johnson. So is Curt Schilling. The difference is that Kobe and Magic didn't presume that their brilliance and success in sports—or the hobbies they were personally enthusiastic about—qualified them to make multimillion-dollar investment decisions. So they educated themselves and sought out the best financial minds to partner with. That's smart. You need good advisors and experts because like the rest of us, you have blind spots.

Michael Huyghue, former commissioner of the now defunct United Football League, told Action News Jacksonville of Brunell, "He's trusting, and maybe that's a weakness. Athletes are at the highest end of the risk spectrum. When you think about what they do for a living, the risks they take with their bodies and their lives to go and play the game—so they are more inclined to want to agree to the most high-risk investments. The consequences when they are wrong can be really debilitating."

Vince Papale married his expert. His story ended up becoming a movie starring Mark Wahlberg, but it was in 1992, years after retiring, that he made the move that ensured his financial future. Vince said in our interview:

> I got in with a company that was financed by Banco Popular out of Puerto Rico with—I'm getting bad with names; I think I took too many hits to the head—Tim Fitzpatrick, who eventually became the CEO of Sallie Mae. Tim brought me along as one of his top wholesale mortgage guys. I was very successful, and I was pretty much doing that when I met [my wife,] Janet. She was a realtor at that time and had a substantial portfolio of her own.
>
> We got married, and then we transferred our portfolio over to somebody, and they pissed it away. So then we're starting from scratch, but nobody knew real estate in Philadelphia better than Janet. So we invested. We invested in several properties, eight of them in total. Today, we have six of them and they have been quite successful.

THE BIGGEST MISTAKE A PRO ATHLETE CAN MAKE

But making reckless investment decisions or choosing to forego the advice of the experts in areas like capital markets and real estate aren't actually the worst financial mistakes a professional athlete can make. They're bad, but another tops the list. The worst money mistake a pro athlete can make is:

They assume there will always be a "next" contract.

This applies even if you're an individual competitor because most athletes in sports like golf and cycling make a majority of their income off of endorsement deals with consumer brands and sponsorship deals with brands that make the equipment they use in their sport. In either case, the income of a pro athlete is always much more precarious than it seems.

Look at what happened to the 2020 Major League Baseball season because of the COVID-19 pandemic. In the end, the season was cut to sixty games, all players accepted prorated fractions of their salaries, and the league as a whole lost $3.1 billion, leading to serious questions about how much players might be able to get from free agency in the future. But you don't need anything as dramatic or historic as a global pandemic to suddenly terminate your ability to earn an income. That can happen in many prosaic ways:

- **Injury.** No details required here. You already know how quickly a wrong step, a bad pivot in the key, an inside fastball, or a savage sack can instantly end a career.

- **Changes to your sport.** Ever see the classic movie *Slap Shot*, with Paul Newman? It's about the ups and downs of a ragtag hockey team that wins its fans hearts with its savage, violent play. The thing is, that was an accurate reflection of the NHL in the 1970s. Teams had a designated "goon" whose main job was to fight with the guys on the other team. But no longer. The NHL has cleaned up its act: fighting has dropped by about two-thirds. That means players with marginal skills whose only talent was beating other players to a pulp no longer have jobs. You can apply the same idea to fullbacks in football, back-to-the-basket low-post centers in basketball, and all-glove, no-bat shortstops in baseball. When sports evolve, some players become expendable.

- **Age.** All major sports are getting younger. As biomechanical science and data-based performance metrics supersede scouting instincts for evaluating players (one wonders if greats like Steve Nash or Greg Maddux would even be drafted today), youth and athleticism become more important.

- **Cost.** Factors like free agency and luxury tax thresholds can make teams extremely cost-conscious. If you've signed an expensive contract and your salary has become a burden for your team, you might not be offered another one.

- **Scandals and legal trouble.** Superstars like Barry Bonds and Lance Armstrong have lost millions in endorsement dollars after major scandals, but some players—Vikings tackle Bryant McKinnie, NBA player Roy Tarpley, MLB outfielder Milton Bradley, to name just a few—have seen their careers and earnings cut drastically short because they just couldn't behave.

The danger for pro athletes is complacency. The peak earning window for an athlete can be incredibly brief and incredibly volatile, and athletes who say to themselves, "I don't need to save because when I retire I'll still make big bucks from endorsements and a TV deal" are dangerously naive. The reality is that most retired professional athletes, even if they're fortunate enough to land lucrative broadcasting contracts or endorsement deals after their playing careers are over, will never again make the kind of money they made when they were playing. That can come as a shock.

According to Athlete Wealth Management, the average professional athlete will earn between 70 and 90 percent of his or her lifetime earnings before age forty. Remember our example from the last chapter. You may have to pay for fifty years of post-career life with an annual income that, unless you invest and plan extremely well, is a fraction of what you earned each year during your playing days.

Of course, you could assume that you're an outlier, one of those athletes who'll walk into a lucrative broadcasting job or book deal after retirement, but in my business, we don't bet on outliers. Outliers are rare. The athletes who enjoy high standards of living, financial security, and real wealth after their playing days are over are the ones who don't assume there's another contract coming and start making plans for the future *now*. My job, your job, and the job of your financial team is to create and execute a plan that turns your inevitable post-career earnings drop into a relaxing glide, not a plunge into an abyss.

We do that by doing two things: investing early and following a sound financial DIET.

KNOW THE SCORE

The Tepper Ratio

Start building your lifetime financial strategy around what I modestly call the **Tepper Ratio**. Your earnings as an active athlete—including endorsements—should make up no more than 50 percent of your lifetime earnings. Put another way, plan so that your pretax earnings from retirement to age seventy are at least equal to what you earned in your career.

Why seventy? Because that's the ideal age to access assets such as qualified retirement accounts or league pensions. The longer you leave that money untouched, the more you'll have. So if you earn $15 million in your playing career and retire at forty, according to the Tepper Ratio, you need to develop a plan that enables you to earn another $15 million over the next thirty years. Those earnings could come from any source: salary, endorsements, book royalties, licensing of your name and likeness, capital gains, dividends, rent from income properties, you name it. An income of $15 million over thirty years is $600,000 a year before taxes, and if you've been disciplined about savings and debt, you can live nicely on that. But the only way to make this happen is to take action now.

START SAVING EARLY

The first thing smart athletes do is invest early in their careers, before they've bought expensive homes and built lavish lifestyles. Investing early also lets you take maximum advantage of the wealth-building power of compound interest, about which Albert Einstein once said, "Compound interest is the eighth wonder of the world. He who understands it, earns it . . . he who doesn't . . . pays it."

If you're a young athlete looking at a big windfall—a signing bonus, for example—the easiest and smartest thing to do would be to invest 100 percent of the net on day one of your career and live off of your salary. Here's what that looks like.

You're a twenty-two-year-old mid–first round NFL draft pick, and you sign a four-year, $14 million contract with a guaranteed $8 million signing bonus. You play out your entire contract (i.e., you don't get cut) and realize the full value of the contract. We'll assume your $6 million in salary is paid at $1.5 million per year. The easiest, smartest thing to do would be to invest 100 percent of your net signing bonus on day one and live off your salary. If your net signing bonus (after fees, commissions, and taxes) is $4 million and your CFO invests it right away, here's what that pot of money would look like at a 7 percent annualized rate of return:

- Five years—$5.6 million
- Ten years—$7.8 million
- Twenty years—$15.5 million

Imagine being only forty-two years old, retired, with your whole life ahead of you, and $15 million sitting in the bank ready to put to work. You're still more than twenty years shy of the typical retirement age in the US, but you've got plenty of money to fund those years.

What does that same plan look like after retirement? Let's see. (I put this kind of plan together for my athlete clients all the time, but this one is *extremely* simplified.) Suppose you play from age twenty-two to thirty-two. You follow the above plan and have about $7.8 million in assets when you retire. From age thirty-two to sixty (close to the typical retirement age), you're "semiretired." You can use some of the assets in your portfolio to *subsidize* (but not completely fund) your lifestyle.

That means you'll need a source of income after retiring, which could be broadcasting, managing a real estate portfolio, overseeing franchises, speaking, or other.

I'll let you use 2 percent of your portfolio's value annually over the course of those twenty-eight years—adjusted for inflation—to subsidize your lifestyle. In this example, that equals about $150,000 per year. If you earn $350,000 a year from your other ventures, you'll have a pretax annual income of about $500,000. That's one-third of what you made when you were playing, but if you keep your debt low and clamp down on extravagant spending, you'll be fine.

Keep in mind that the more you subsidize your income, the less you'll have in later years. In this example, you're spending 2 percent of your assets per year, so you won't realize 7 percent annualized growth on the total—you'll get 5 percent growth. But even a 5 percent return over twenty-eight years gets you to $30 million at age sixty.

Now, at age sixty, you're retired. In retirement, you can live off 3 percent of your portfolio, or $900,000 per year before taxes. If you start collecting a pension from your league or player's union, that number is even higher. So now you're still middle-aged, hopefully healthy, with years of freedom ahead of you and an annual income approaching one million dollars, not that much less than you were making as a player. Sounds pretty good, doesn't it?

THE ATHLETE INCOME PLANNER

I mentioned this tool early in the book, and now it's time to use it. The Athlete Income Planner (AIP) is a free software application you'll find at WealthLit101.com (the same place you'll find my Financial Literacy for Athletes bite-sized video learning program). Just plug in variables like where you live, your age, salary, signing bonus, and what percentages of your income you want to allocate for living expenses and investing. In real time the AIP calculates how much you'll pay in taxes and the returns and income your savings will produce for you all the way up to age ninety. Play around—raise or lower the amount you live on or save—and watch how the numbers change. It's a fantastic tool for seeing how the financial decisions you make while you're playing can affect your quality of life in twenty-five years.

Go to WealthLit101.com and start seeing how your numbers look!

THE INGREDIENTS IN YOUR FINANCIAL DIET

The second key to a prosperous post-career life is having a lifetime financial road map, following that map with ruthless discipline, and changing direction as your situation and needs change. Now, everybody has an acronym these days, so I created DIET. DIET stands for the four key ingredients in your financial plan:

- **Discipline**: How well you save, avoid debt, and pay your taxes.
- **Investments**: The diversified portfolio of instruments where you'll put your money.
- **Education**: Learning about finance and business so you're not entirely dependent on your team.
- **Team**: A group that includes your Board of Directors, the people who advise you, identify opportunities, and hold you accountable.

The idea of putting together a financial road map for the next fifty years of your life can seem overwhelming, so much so that you might be tempted to just hand someone the keys and say, "Here, you drive. Just send me quarterly statements." That's why I have an acronym and why I don't call your financial plan a road map, blueprint, or any of those other tired names. I compare it to a nutritional diet because:

- Like a nutritional diet, you get out of it exactly what you put into it.
- Like a nutritional diet, it requires discipline but must also allow for the real world.

- Like a nutritional diet, it's made up of a few critical ingredients.
- As a professional athlete, you're already accustomed to paying close attention to what you put in your body, so this just makes sense.

Let's look at the ingredients in an athlete's healthy financial DIET.

D = DISCIPLINE

The first item on our list of ingredients is *savings*. Saving money isn't sexy—it's a lot hotter to take your significant other out and pay cash for a Ferrari you don't need—but it is the cornerstone of every athlete's future well-being. When you are interviewing potential members of your financial team, saving, budgeting, and controlling monthly spending should be the *first* topic they bring up, not hedge funds and options contracts. If they don't want to talk about savings, talk with someone else.

In saving, you're building two pots of money:

- Emergency savings you can tap when something goes very wrong.
- The money you will invest for the long term.

For emergency funds, set a target to save 30 percent of your net income with every paycheck you receive, and do the same with any endorsement, licensing, or personal appearance income. (We've also discussed athletes who save 100 percent of their bonuses or salaries and live on their endorsement income, and that's a great option as well.) Save 30 percent of your income until your total savings equals one year's worth of expenses (note that I'm talking about essential expenses like food and the mortgage, not discretionary spending). That money goes into a special account, and you don't touch it. You'll live off the other 70 percent of your income.

Now comes the savings plan I mentioned briefly back in Chapter Three, only now we're going to dig into the details. When you have saved one year's worth of expenses, stop depositing funds into your emergency account. You're going divide up your income differently, using 35 to 40 percent of your net income to cover your living expenses and investing the remaining 60 to 65 percent in things like stocks, mutual funds, and real estate. That's how you'll build your long-term wealth while living a comfortable but not extravagant lifestyle.

To facilitate all this saving, have your CFO set up a high-yield checking account that will become your main bank account, the account from which your purchases, transfers, charges, and fees are debited. Every time you're paid, your money will transfer into that account via direct deposit. Every month funds will transfer out of that account automatically to cover things like routine expenses, debt payments, taxes, and investments. Have your CFO research various high-yield accounts' fees, services, accessibility of funds, and the solidity of the banks that manage them and then recommend the best primary account.

This is the opportunity to become accustomed to a lifestyle that is comfortable but not exorbitant. Once you get accustomed to a lavish lifestyle, it's hard to go back. So choose a comfortable lifestyle where you can do most of what you want to do, but not a crazy one where you're spending recklessly. Long-term freedom comes from having a plan that works in a good market and a bad market and sticking to it. Does this mean you can't buy a second home in a couple of years or buy your mom a place? Of course not, but it does mean you have to start setting aside money for those purchases. Following this strategy over the long term means you're not impulsive about your finances. Example:

Suppose you're a solid PGA Tour pro golfer making about $3 million a year in tournament prizes and endorsements. You're not Tiger Woods, but you're not starving either. You're only taking home $1.5 million because the rest is going to federal, state, and local taxes, along with commissions paid to your agent.

Now let's say you have a reasonably comfortable lifestyle, and your annual expenses are $400,000. If you follow the DIET plan, you'll put 75 percent of that $1.5 million in net income into an emergency account until the balance reaches $400,000, which will take about four-and-a-half months. Meanwhile, you'll live off the other 25 percent. Your goal is to have one year's worth of expenses in cash-type accounts where the money is liquid and safe.

Once that's done, your income allocation will change. Your COO will set aside 35 percent of your $1.5 million net income—around $500,000—and use it to pay all your living expenses. That's the money you'll use to eat out, pay your caddy, swing coach, and personal trainer, and do whatever else you want to do. You'll also have some "mad money" left for small extravagances and luxuries, like renting a villa somewhere tropical. That's just over $41,600 per month. If you can't live on that, you might want to reread Chapter Six, because your spending is seriously out of control.

Meanwhile, your CFO will allocate the remaining 65 percent, which we'll round up to $1 million, and put it into familiar investments such as an IRA or 401(k), mutual funds, index funds, or individual stocks, as well as real estate, hedge funds (which are generally open only to high-income investors), and venture capital. (If you want to have some extra fun, spend 40 percent on your lifestyle, as long as you invest the other 60 percent. Investing is your permission slip for spending a little extra on a nice car or a luxury vacation.)

Here's how it breaks down:

Pretax annual income:	$3 million
Income after taxes:	$1.5 million
Investment savings pot:	$1 million/year
Living expenses pot:	$500,000/year

Here's where it gets good. If you compete at a high level for just six years—say, from age twenty-five to thirty—and you stay with this program, you'll have $400,000 in your emergency account (plus some interest), and if you assume a 7 percent annualized return, about $9.1 million in principal and returns from your investments. Even if you hang up your clubs at thirty, you're positioned perfectly for your next act and for the next forty years of your life.

Your CFO will recommend a portfolio of investments for you based on your income, age, goals, and the costs associated with each, but there are a few guidelines that are universal no matter where you're investing your money:

- **Diversify, diversify, diversify.** Your money should be in a broad range of types of securities, funds, and other instruments. Diversification is a proven way to reduce risk while increasing return.

- **Open a retirement account.** One place your money should be is in a qualified retirement account like a 401(k) plan. These are tax-deferred accounts that you cannot access until you are at least 59.5 years old, and over a period of decades, with regular contributions, their balances can grow to the millions. That's a nice backstop to have in your sixties.

- **Take advantage of team or league retirement programs.** Many sports leagues offer pensions or will match the contributions you make to your own retirement accounts. If they do, be sure to take advantage. Otherwise you're turning away free money.

- **Pay attention to fees.** Sometimes, dazzling investments don't look as good when you take their fees into account. Two percent may not seem like much at the time, but over thirty years, a 2 percent fee can have a substantial impact on the value of an investment portfolio (see the Know the Score sidebar in this chapter).

- **Build your portfolio and then ignore it.** The biggest mistake investors can make is to watch their portfolio's value daily or the latest news on the Dow or S&P 500. Markets rise and fall; that's what they do. However, the US stock market has been a consistent creator of wealth for more than two centuries, and I don't see that changing in the long term. When stocks plummeted after the scope of the coronavirus pandemic became clear, I had one overarching piece of advice for my clients: *Relax.* Selling when the market is down just turns paper losses into actual losses. The best thing to do is use those so-called "pullbacks" as an opportunity to reposition your portfolio, but leave that to the experts.

Often, the best thing to do is nothing. Sure enough, I had my clients sit tight and not take rash action, and some even bought while prices were low. As I write this, the stock market has recovered all its lost ground—and then some. Build your portfolio, and then forget about it.

You never know when having some money saved will save your ass. Financial advisor Brandon Averill told me in our interview, which took place in the middle of the free fall of the financial markets, that his insistence on saving really benefited his clients during the COVID-19 postponement of the MLB season.

We caught some flack, and it's been a competitive negative for us that we harp so heavily on setting aside money in a very conservative way for a period like this. We really pushed our clients not to expose a pretty large amount of their money to unnecessary risks so there wasn't a major disruption in their earnings because of something like a career-ending injury or just not being good. I mean, it's hard to make money in sports. On the low end, we were setting aside two years of living expenses, and some of our minor league guys were doing up to five years of living expenses in a treasury portfolio. So the money is going to be there when you need it. Let's just say that we're not getting a whole lot of pushback on that now. We have zero clients panicking right now.

Personally, I'm in favor of having more of your money working for you, which means it's invested in markets and not sitting in a savings account earning less than 1 percent interest. Saving an emergency fund to cover one year of essential expenses should be sufficient.

KNOW THE SCORE

Don't overlook the effect of fees on your investment returns. Let's say you have an investment account with a beginning balance of $1 million invested over twenty years and you earn an 8 percent return before fees. According to the Securities and Exchange Commission, if you paid a fee of 1 percent over those twenty years, the net value or your portfolio would be $3.8 million. If you increased the fee to 2 percent, the same portfolio would be worth $3.2 million. That additional percentage point in fees would cost you $600,000.

What are reasonable fees for financial services? It depends on what's included in the services you receive, but this is a general guideline:

- Up to $1 million under management = maximum fee of 1.25 percent
- $1 million–$5 million = maximum fee of 1 percent
- $5+ million = maximum fee of 0.8 percent

DEBT

One of the blessings of being a professional athlete is that everyone will extend you credit because you have the income to make payments. And one of the curses of being a professional athlete is that everyone will extend you credit because you have the income to make payments. Yeah, it's a double-edged sword all right. Debt is necessary, but potentially dangerous, because it's invisible. That's why earlier I suggested only using prepaid debit cards when you go out in order to control spending; when you can't see the money leaving your hand, it becomes easy to overextend yourself.

There are a few factors that make debt something to be very careful about. First and foremost, all debt comes with interest payments. You know, your Visa card comes with an interest rate of 15.9 percent (yes, credit card rates are insane), your car loan has an interest rate of 4.9 percent, and you borrowed money for your mortgage at 3.5 percent because money is incredibly cheap right now. What all those numbers mean is that over time, you're going to pay a lot more for the things you buy with debt than the actual cost of those things:

- If you have a $20,000 balance on a credit card with an interest rate of 18 percent, and you pay $1,000 a month in payments, by the time you pay off that balance (assuming you don't use the card again at all), you'll pay an extra $3,956.54 in interest.

- If you buy an $80,000 car and finance $60,000 of the cost at 4.9 percent over five years, you'll pay an extra $7,772 in interest.

- If you buy a $1 million home and finance $800,000 of the price at 3.5 percent over 30 years, you will end up paying a whopping $493,249 in interest.

Maintaining debt over the long term can cost you thousands of dollars that you never know you're losing because it's rolled into your monthly payments. However, that's not the biggest trap that debt can lay for you. If you read the stories of athletes who've squandered huge amounts of money from their playing days, one of the common patterns is going into debt for huge homes, real estate investments, and businesses without the money to pay them back if anything goes sideways. In other words, their ability to stay current on that $3 million mortgage and pay debt service on the $2 million loan they took out to open a bar depends on their life and career going perfectly. If you take nothing else away from this book, take this:

Betting on life going perfectly is always a bad bet.

Shit happens. Athletes get hurt, slow down, get cut. Suddenly, you're millions in the red and your income is gone. That's why I advise my athlete clients to be very careful about the temptations of debt. On your DIET, debt is like a donut shop. You might intend to take just one bite of a glazed, but it's soooo good, and before you know it, you've binged and eaten half the store. Debt gets you things that you want, things that make you feel good, but there's always a price to be paid.

Here are some good rules to follow about debt:

- People will talk about "good debt" like it's something that warrants an attaboy. But in my experience, there is no good debt. There's only "less bad" debt. Less bad debts are debts that enable you to increase your wealth over time. They include taking out a mortgage to buy a home or other real estate, taking out a student loan (because getting a college degree increases your earning power), taking out a loan to start a small business, and sometimes, borrowing against your home to perform renovations that increase its value. Some of these debts can be worth taking on, but they should all be handled with care. It might be good to buy a home, but it's stupid to buy a $5 million mansion for four people when you have an athlete's volatile income and no savings.

- Good debt does two things: it buys you appreciating assets that have *positive arbitrage*. Arbitrage is a fancy word that means the difference between the income you get from something and what it costs you. If your investment portfolio is earning 7 percent and you finance your house at 3 percent rather than cashing out your investments to pay cash, you would have a positive arbitrage of 4 percent and would grow your wealth over time by opting for the mortgage.

- Some debt can make sense when it's in the context of growing a business, such as a business line of credit at a bank or convertible debt (when business owners borrow money from investors that is later converted to equity in the company). However, those are complex financial instruments that should only be used with the advice of an expert financial team.

- Bad debt is basically any other type of debt, especially debt for consumption and for depreciating assets like cars and boats. Minimize your credit card debt, which grows and comes with ridiculous interest rates, as you've seen. Avoid bad debt whenever possible. Pay your credit card balances in full each month and ignore come-ons to sign up for new cards or take out cash advances.

- If you're disciplined, you can finance purchases like a house. If you're not disciplined, pay cash if you can. You will avoid missed or late payments that will damage your credit scores.

TEPPER TIP

Consider protecting your identity and credit information from thieves by freezing your credit reports with the three big credit bureaus. With the reports frozen, no one can run a credit check on you without it being flagged and no one can open a new credit account in your name. If you don't plan on financing a home or car anytime soon, a credit freeze is like a bulletproof vest for your credit scores.

HOW TRUSTWORTHY ARE YOU?

Apart from running up huge, hidden financial obligations that grow over time, debt has another negative effect: carrying too much of it will lower your credit score. You might be familiar with the FICO score, that number ranging from 300 to 850 that each adult has associated with his or her Social Security number. Your FICO score is a composite number representing your credit history as compiled by the three independent credit bureaus: Experian, Equifax, and TransUnion. These companies keep a record of how responsible you are at using credit: how often you pay your debts on time, how much of your credit limit you use, how often you apply for loans, and so on. Your FICO score basically measures how financially trustworthy you are.

Carrying a great deal of debt, or worse, defaulting on some of that debt, can do a number on your FICO score, which can really hurt you when you're trying to build your life after sports. Suppose you're approaching the end of your playing career and you're looking to buy some restaurant franchises as a way to grow wealth. Or you're looking to purchase some rental properties. If potential creditors look at your credit history and see that your FICO score has dropped from 750 to 620 in the last two years because of unpaid credit card bills and a car repossession, they're likely to conclude that you're a poor risk and deny you a loan.

In other words, taking on debt you're unsure about paying back can directly affect your financial future. Instead of doing that, follow these few simple rules:

- Avoid debt completely if you can. If you're cash rich and want something, pay cash for it.

- If you have to take out loans for a purchase, take out a loan for the shortest possible term and pay it off as quickly as you can. Money is cheap right now, and there might be some tax advantages in taking out a mortgage to purchase a home (talk with your tax advisor about this), but if you do, consider a fifteen- or ten-year note. You'll pay more per month but pay the house off more quickly and save hundreds of thousands in interest.

- Watch your debt-to-income ratio. That's the percentage of your monthly pretax income that's committed to debt payments. So if your monthly gross income is $50,000 and you have $20,000 in payments to loans and credit cards, your debt-to-income ratio is 40 percent. Some lenders say that's acceptable, but it's not acceptable for an athlete with a volatile income. I suggest that you keep your debt-to-income ratio no higher than 20 percent. That way, if something happens to curtail your income, your savings will allow you to take care of your obligations, avoid default and bankruptcy, and protect your credit score.

And the most important rule of all:

Think twice about taking on debt you don't already have the assets to pay back.

Failure to follow this rule is what sinks so many athletes who've made millions in their careers but wind up bankrupt. They take on debt to purchase assets in the hope that the assets will increase in value, enabling them to pay off the debt when it comes due. This concept is called *leverage*—using borrowed money to buy assets you plan to use to pay back the loan. In the right hands, it's a useful financial tool. But in the wrong hands, it can lead to disaster. Avoid it as much as possible. When you can, only take on debt when you already have enough cash on hand or guaranteed income to repay the loan in case something goes bad.

Does that mean that early in your career, you might not be able to buy a house? Possibly. If you're only making $500,000 this season but have signed a guaranteed contract paying you $25 million over the next five seasons, that's as good as money in the bank. Same thing for guaranteed endorsement contracts. As long as you don't violate the contract, you have the money and can take on the debt. But if your near the end of your career and there's no new contract, limit your debt to the amount of dividends and interest being thrown off by your investment portfolio. That way, you're never dipping into your principal to service debt.

FROM THE ATHLETE

Merril Hoge, Former NFL Running Back and Broadcaster, on Taking Advice

"Journalist Kendall Bell told me a story about a kid from Pitt who got a $500,000 signing bonus. He gets his check in the mail and sees its for about $287,000. He calls the Steelers and says, 'Where's the rest of the money?' They told him about taxes, FICA, all that. He knew nothing about taxes. He didn't understand that he had to pay taxes.

"I was doing the rookie symposium. It's a presentation about all resources that are available to you. My panel was two rookies just sitting in those chairs, and we covered a bunch of subjects from managing money to tickets, friends, the lifestyle, and the workload. This kid stands up, this wide receiver from Pitt, points, and goes, 'Man, yo, fuck you, fuck you, motherfucker. You ain't telling me what to do with my money!'

"I was like, 'Hey, time-out. Nobody's telling you what to do with it. They're telling you what they experienced and just giving you a heads up about what's coming. You do what you want to do with your money, how you see fit. They're just trying to give you some guidance that you could use.'

"He says, 'Fuck you, fuck the NFL, fuck the Dallas Cowboys. I'm taking care of my boys!' The whole thing almost turned into a freaking brawl. It just really opened my eyes to just some of the ignorance and incompetence that's out there."

TAXES

I'll spare you the "death and taxes" thing. Taxes are a reality for all pro athletes, but they're one that too many athletes are unprepared for. Apart from the simple fact that federal, state, and local income taxes take such a large bite out of athletes' take-home pay, the biggest issue with athletes and their taxes is how mind-numbingly complex they can be.

As K. Sean Packard writes in *Forbes*, "Not every state uses the same calculation to determine what portion of an athlete's income to tax, and some use different calculations based on the sport. For example, Pennsylvania taxes baseball, basketball, and hockey players on the ratio games in the state over total games played, including pre- and postseason, but they tax football players based on days worked in the state over total days worked. Michigan uses the same method but excludes the preseason. Most other states use the days worked method. Arizona uses that method but excludes days worked in the preseason."

Okay, I'm confused, and I'm in this business! Athletes also receive different types of income that are classified by the IRS in different ways. The salary you receive from a team is classified as wages, and you receive a W-2 for those, just like you would if you worked at a factory or bank. If you're a professional tennis player, you're an independent contractor, and you'll receive 1099 forms for all your tournament winnings. However, athletes working for a league and individual performers like golfers and tennis players also get 1099s for income from sources like endorsements, sponsorships, and speaking engagements. So yes, every successful athlete has a very skilled CPA toiling behind the scenes to make sure documents are properly compiled and filed.

THE "JOCK TAX"

But that's just the tip of the iceberg. There's also the bane of the athlete's existence, the so-called "jock tax" (see the Time-Out sidebar later in this chapter). Basically, athletes have to pay taxes on income they earn in every jurisdiction in which they earn the income. That means if you're on a pro team that plays in multiple US states, you have to pay state income tax on the money you earn in those states and file a tax return for that state. If you're a golfer, marathoner, or other soloist who competes overseas, you have to pay tax on winnings you earn in those countries according to those countries' tax laws.

Oh, and if the city you play in also levies a city earnings tax, as many cities do, you have to pay that as well. As a result MLB players can end up paying income taxes in twenty to twenty-five jurisdictions, NBA players typically pay in sixteen to twenty jurisdictions, and NFL players have to file between ten and twelve returns. And while your earnings from playing your sport are taxed where you earn the money, income from things like endorsements, personal appearances, dividends, and interest is taxed in your state of residence. Athlete tax preparation is why some enrolled agents and CPAs have dark circles under their eyes year-round.

Oh, there's more. Tax laws are constantly changing, and some of those changes impact what athletes pay. For example, the 2017 Tax Cuts and Jobs Act capped the federal tax deduction for state and local taxes paid at $10,000. Players who reside in high-tax states like New York and California might pay state and local taxes in excess of $50,000 a year and before 2018 would have been able to deduct some of those taxes on their federal tax return. So the new cap has cost players money. That's one example showing why working with tax experts who specialize in tax planning and preparation for athletes is essential.

Tax planning involves numerous decisions designed to minimize your tax obligation within the confines of the law, including when you get your income, when you make certain purchases, the debt you take on, when you make expenditures, the type of retirement plans and investments you choose, and many other variables. Given the complexity of athletes' tax situation, tax planning is extremely important not only for maximizing the amount of money you keep but also for avoiding costly penalties and interest for underpayment of taxes.

Averill explains:

Tax prep for athletes can be very complex. But more influential is the tax planning. If you don't have integrated tax advice in your financial model, clients are typically being shortchanged. Really understanding how athlete taxes work and how multistate taxation works is absolutely critical to a successful outcome for athlete clients. For instance, in baseball, the teams allocate wages based upon the one-hundred-and-sixty-two-game schedule. But what isn't taken into account is the time they spend in spring training or other team-mandated days.

So you need a tax team that really understands that and can reallocate those wages and do so in a way that is defensible in a tax audit. The planning side is a whole different ball of wax. Structuring of contracts and all that stuff makes a huge difference. Signing bonuses, upfront versus timing of payments—taxes just hit every single piece of an athlete's financial life.

For example, one aspect of tax planning that affects pro athletes more than most people is your legal state of residence. That doesn't have to be the state your team plays in; establishing residence usually means you've bought a house in a state or spend substantial off-season time there. (Registering to vote or getting a driver's license in a state does *not* make you a legal resident.) If you play for a team in Nashville, you can still establish residence in Florida. The advantage of doing so is that states like Florida and Texas don't have a state income tax.

Your legal place of residence can have a big effect on your tax obligation, says Averill. "For instance, if you're a California resident, you're going to pay north of 13 percent in state tax," he says. "Let's say you played for the Texas Rangers, and they're not allocating half of your wages to Texas because there's no state income tax there. That's not excluded from your California wages. You're going to pay the California tax no matter what. Take that California resident and move him to Texas, and he's immediately going to save more than 13 percent on half of his wages. That's a huge impact, and it's all about where you live."

DISCIPLINE, TAX SAVINGS ACCOUNTS, AND EXPERT HELP

The discipline part comes into the tax discussion when we talk about *estimated taxes*. If you're paid a salary by your team, those taxes are taken out of your paycheck; you don't have to worry about them. But like I said, income from sources like endorsements is treated like income to an independent contractor, which means taxes aren't deducted from those checks. You're responsible for paying those taxes yourself four times a year. Those are estimated or quarterly taxes. To make sure those get paid on time and you avoid big penalties, set up a *tax savings account* where you deposit 25 to 30 percent of your 1099 earnings. That way, your CPA can easily pay your estimated taxes on time every January 15, April 15, June 15, and September 15.

But the two most important things to know about your taxes are to always make sure they're paid and to always get expert assistance with tax planning and preparation. As you've seen, tax planning for pro athletes is insanely complicated; you'll need your CFO and CPA to team up on the planning, and you'll probably need a team of experienced tax experts to prepare and file all your returns. Just remember this. Tax *avoidance* is legal, but tax *evasion* will land you in prison.

For example, Filipino boxing legend Manny Pacquiao spent years battling the US government and the government of the Philippines over $18 million in unpaid taxes to the IRS and a whopping $75 million the Philippines government said it was owed. As of 2019, after liens and account seizures, the fight was still ongoing. Don't cross the line with taxes. Use every legal measure you and your CFO can to minimize your tax obligation, then pay what you owe.

TIME-OUT

More on the "Jock Tax"

Does the "jock tax," in which athletes have to pay tax on some of their income to the states or cities where they play, actually cost athletes money? Overall, yes. Smart tax planning can help players avoid paying state income taxes on endorsements and other 1099 income by doing things like deferring salary or maximizing unique athlete deductions. But the jock tax can also screw you. For example, if you live in a state with a state income tax, you can get a credit on your state taxes for the tax you pay in other states. But if you live in a nontax state, you won't get that credit. "If you live in Florida, the taxes you pay to those other states is really taking money out of your pocket because you're not going to get a credit for those state taxes," says CPA Robert Raiola. "If you live in a nontax state, you could easily end up paying state tax on 60 to 65 percent of your earned income from the team, even though you don't have a tax in the state you reside in." Because tax preparation and filing can be incredibly complex for athletes, you'll probably pay more for tax prep and accounting services. No QuickBooks for you.

I = INVESTMENTS

The I in DIET represents your **investments**, the financial instruments you use to grow your wealth and build a lifetime of predictable income. Your CFO will work with you to build a diversified portfolio of investments that give you the greatest tax advantage and effectively balance volatility with rate of return. At the risk of oversimplifying, you will typically learn about four major investment terms when you sit down with your financial advisor:

1. **Retirement Accounts.** You've heard of IRAs, 401(k)s, and similar qualified retirement accounts. Investing in them is a no-brainer for pro athletes, and you should open such an account as early as possible in your career because the more time you give your money to grow, the more you'll have when you retire. Even better, many of these accounts are tax-deferred, so making an annual contribution

to your IRA reduces your income tax obligation.

Since many pro athletes have more than one kind of income, you might also be able to open more than one qualified retirement account. You can contribute to a 401(k) plan as a salaried employee of your team, but since you also get endorsement income as an independent contractor, you can also contribute to what's known as a SEP-IRA. The 401(k) annual contribution limit for 2020 is $19,500 per year, while the limit for a SEP-IRA is $57,000.

If you're making millions per year in income, those amounts might not seem like much, but consider this. If you opened a 401(k) when you were twenty-five and contributed $19,500 to it each year until you were sixty-five, and earned an annualized return of 7 percent, you would have $3,892,884. If you opened a SEP-IRA at the same age and contributed $57,000 each year for forty years, you would end up with $11,379,201. That's nothing to sneeze at.

2. **Securities.** These are the financial instruments most people think about when they talk about investing: stocks, bonds, mutual funds, index funds, and exchange traded funds (ETFs).

> » **Stocks** represent fractional ownership shares of a public corporation and are bought and sold on stock exchanges like the New York Stock Exchange.
> » When you purchase **bonds**, you are lending money to public borrowers (like governments) and private borrowers (like corporations) who promise to pay you interest along with returning your principal when the bond matures. Bond investments are generally safer but offer low returns relative to stocks.
> » **Mutual funds** are collections of individual stocks (or bonds) grouped into a single investment vehicle. They offer a high degree of diversification and are extremely popular investment instruments.

> » **Index funds** are mutual funds whose component stocks match those in a particular stock index, such as the S&P 500. So as those indexes rise and fall, so do the value of their index funds.

> » **ETFs** are investment funds that are traded on stock exchanges just like individual stocks. They often track stock indexes as well, like index funds.

3. **High-Net-Worth Investments.** When you pass $5 million in investable funds available, a new world of investment opportunities becomes available to you that are not available to the average investor. These instruments can deliver potentially much higher returns, help reduce your tax obligation, and also reduce your overall risk profile.

> » **Hedge funds** are limited partnerships made up of a group of high-net-worth individuals who pool their money to invest in a broad range of areas not available to most investors, including land, stocks, currency, and real estate investment trusts (REITs). Hedge funds are typically managed aggressively and often use leverage—borrowed money—to invest.

> » **Private equity** pools money from accredited investors (investors who meet certain stringent requirements) or funds that are not publicly listed on any exchange and uses it to directly invest in private companies or engage in buyouts of public corporations.

> » **Venture capital and angel investing** allow individual investors to purchase equity in young and start-up companies seeking early funding. As many start-ups fail, such investments can be risky, but when a new company hits big, these investments can prove extremely lucrative.

4. **Business and Real Estate.** Finally, many athletes choose to invest in businesses and real estate in various forms:

    » **Business investments** can include becoming an equity investor in a private company (purchasing a share of the business), buying into franchises of national brands (often restaurant chains such as Chipotle), and starting your own enterprises, such as clothing brands. Franchising is particularly attractive for ex-athletes; at one point NBA superstar Shaquille O'Neal was invested in 155 Five Guys franchises, 17 Auntie Anne's pretzel locations, 9 Papa John's pizza locations, and 40 branches of 24 Hour Fitness.

    » **Real estate** is another very popular investment for athletes. Real estate investment can take the form of commercial properties, single family rentals, multifamily rentals, retail properties, and even land. Many star athletes have invested big in real estate as a way to build long-term wealth. MLB superstar Alex Rodriguez, for example, began investing in real estate in 2003 when he bought a Florida duplex, and today, his company, Monument Capital Management, has started four housing hedge funds and owns more than $700 million in properties around the country.

If you've ever wondered how some athletes earn more after their lucrative playing careers are over than they did while they were on the field, this is how. *Investments.* Smart, strategic investments made with the help of a team of experts. Franchises, real estate, hedge funds, venture capital, starting their own branded product lines. The smart ones begin investing while they're playing and build mini-empires that continue to grow when they're retired.

E = EDUCATION

Remember former NFL placekicker Doug Brien? When he signed with the NFL's New Orleans Saints in 2000, he was already interested in real estate, but he knew he needed to learn more in order to become a better investor. So he became one of the few active NFL players ever to attend college *during* the season, taking classes at Tulane University and eventually earning his MBA. The education paid off: Brien built a strong portfolio of properties, and his real estate education helped him cofound single family rental pioneer Waypoint Homes.

Education has been critical to Doug's success, as he told me in our interview. "I went to the first ever NFL entrepreneurial workshop at the Wharton School of Business," he says. "It was a three-day workshop. Hundreds of players applied, and they accepted twenty-five to the first class based on a combination of years in the league and nonfootball professional experience. We had access to many of the best professors, like Jeremy Siegel. We learned how to invest, how to start a business, how to manage wealth creation throughout your life, how to run a business. It was really good."

Another pattern you'll notice among financially successful athletes is that they are educated. You owe it to yourself to get a basic financial education, which you can do by taking my Financial Literacy for Athletes series of video courses at WealthLit101.com. You'll find about forty ten-minute videos on topics like spending and saving, credit and debt, investing, taxes, and insurance that will allow you to ask better questions of your team and make better day-to-day decisions about things like credit cards and auto loans.

If you're serious about investing in businesses or real estate, it's worth your while to get an even more rigorous education. You don't necessarily have to go back to school and get your MBA or finance degree; there are many other resources available:

- Harvard Crossover into Business Program.
- Columbia Entrepreneurship Program.

- Tuck Business School Next Step Program at Dartmouth.
- The NFL offers an annual Personal Finance Camp.
- MLB offers its players a clearinghouse of financial tools at mlb.com/player-resource-center/financial-resources.
- Organizations like the Global Financial Literacy Excellence Center (gflec.org), the Center for Financial Inclusion (centerforfinancialinclusion.org), the Money Smart Athlete (moneysmartathlete.com), and Investopedia (investopedia.com) are terrific resources for everything from basic financial literacy to advanced concepts.

You could even do like Solomon Wilcots did and take a job with a financial firm. "In the beginning of my career, I was really pissed," he says. "Here I am, an NFL player, and I've got some people—guys that I graduated with that same year—who have sales jobs and make more money than I do. Right then and there, I knew I wasn't going to make enough money to last me the rest of my life. So I needed to be smart. I went and got a job in a management training program. I worked every year in the off-season while I was a player. I learned about financial products and insurance products."

T = TEAM

Finally, the T in DIET: your team, your Board of Directors. I've talked a great deal about this already, so I won't belabor it. Let me just say that the biggest financial debacles among pro athletes have typically occurred with players who a) didn't get expert advice, b) didn't listen to their advisors, c) had incompetent advisors, or d) were defrauded by their advisors. In other words, take the time to carefully screen and hire a capable CMO, COO, and CFO, along with a skilled CPA and a good attorney who knows about business and investing. Take their advice, and you should be fine.

Give your CFO veto power over everything but your day-to-day financial decisions. Let him or her track every penny spent. Open the accounts your CPA tells you to open. Don't check the performance of your portfolio daily unless you want to drive yourself crazy. Insist on monthly statements and at least an annual sit-down during which you go over them, and ask questions until you're satisfied. With the right team, there will be no leaks in the ship. They'll oversee your investment opportunities and handle your tax planning, insurance needs, charitable planning, estate planning, and everything else you need for a prosperous future.

I haven't talked at length about the need for life, health, disability, and long-term care insurance. I haven't talked about estate planning, which can help you support your family and causes that you care about while enjoying tax benefits. I haven't talked about charitable giving, which many successful athletes like LeBron James love to engage in. That's because the options can become overwhelming.

Better to sit down with your CFO and an insurance specialist and talk about your insurance needs. Better to sit down with an investment banker and discuss how you can expand your portfolio into things like franchises and venture capital. Better to talk with your CFO about your long-term goals and how you'd like to see them reflected in your estate plan. Build a great team, educate yourself, and work together. That's a financial DIET that will have you enjoying great financial health for years.

OVERTIME

Career Ending Insurance

Consider buying permanent total disability insurance, known as "career ending" insurance. This is a disability policy that pays you a lump sum—tax-free—if you get hurt and can no longer play your sport. You can also buy temporary total disability insurance, which typically covers athletes like tennis players and cyclists, who get paid for entering and winning events and earn nothing if they're out for six weeks with a tweaked hamstring. Total disability insurance can be expensive—often several thousand dollars per year for each $1 million of coverage—but if you have a family and business empire depending on your $10 million salary, it could be money well spent.

CHAPTER EIGHT

THE HANDOFF

In 2017, free safety Andre Hal signed a three-year, $15 million contract extension (with a $7 million guarantee) with the NFL's Houston Texans. That year he finished with a career high in tackles. But in 2018, he was diagnosed with non-Hodgkin's lymphoma. After his cancer went into remission, he played in about half of the 2018 season, but by then, he'd started questioning his life in football.

In 2019, at only twenty-seven years old and in just the fifth year of his career, Andre retired from football, saying that he didn't want to just collect a check when his heart wasn't in the game. What do you do when you retire from your life's pursuit at an age when most people are just getting started? How do you make that work when you're leaving so much earning potential on the table?

Andre said in our interview:

> "I had a financial advisor at the end of my career. I didn't have one at the beginning. I didn't have that much money to manage anyway, so I didn't need one. That's why I learned how to manage my own money. But when I was thinking about retirement, I needed somebody to crunch the numbers down

for me and make sure I was doing the right thing. My financial advisor is actually one of my best friends. He went to Vanderbilt with me. Before I retired, we had a probably two-hour talk and went over all my finances, and he told me I was good to go. I did a great job with saving my money and not just splurging on stuff I didn't need."

Andre also knew he couldn't depend on someone to do something he wasn't prepared to do for himself, so he started learning about finance.

"Bought a couple of books, like *Rich Dad Poor Dad*. I was just learning about money and trying to figure out how to manage my stuff and do it the right way and not just listen to people. I wanted to learn for myself. Everybody has their own opinion about what you should do with your money. But at the end of the day, you got to know what to do yourself. I made sure I knew what to do. It worked out for me, because I'm financially stable right now, because I did the right things. Even before I had the money, I knew what to do with it. You know what I mean? I wouldn't just splurge it away."

Andre also talked candidly about resisting the so-called "black tax" that a lot of African American athletes feel pressured to pay.

"I think the term came from South Africa, and it refers to the financial support that black professionals are expected to give their extended families. Basically, you're supposed to take care of your family. A lot of black athletes go through that. That's why a lot of black athletes go broke before they know it, because they're taking care of their whole family, and everybody wants a Mercedes. Everybody wants a Range Rover. But everybody can't take care of a Range Rover. It costs probably one thousand dollars every time you get maintenance, you know what I mean? So the athlete ends up paying for that, too. A lot of guys don't realize that until it's too late.

"I told my family no a lot. You know what I mean? If you let somebody live off of you, that means they've got to live off you for the rest of their life. They will stop working. I told my family, "I don't want you to stop working. I don't want you to think that I'm just going to take care of you. I'm going to help you." I helped a lot of my family, but I didn't take care of them. That's why I pretty much kept most of my money."

TEPPER TIP

If you're going to give money to friends and family, make sure it comes out of the 35 or 40 percent of your after-tax income set aside for living expenses, not your investment pot or your emergency funds. This way, you'll need to consciously make a decision to forego luxuries for yourself to help others.

Because he was smart with his money, and because he'd gotten paid most of his $7 million guarantee and saved most of it, Andre was in position to do what he wanted: retire and move on to the next phase of his life. He knew what smart athletes everywhere know: *Money is freedom.* Today he's attending the University of Houston to earn his MBA, he owns his home plus an Airbnb property, and he's investing in businesses prudently and carefully. He could teach a lot of older athletes a few things about retiring right.

One piece of advice he offered:

Say no a lot. I don't think people understand how much pressure that comes on you when you start making money. Everybody feels like you're supposed to help everybody out, but you can't help everyone out. You've got to understand this is what you have to live off of for the rest of your life. Make the money, and save some of it.

It's not bad to splurge sometimes. But splurge on yourself. Don't splurge on your buddies and your mom and your dad and your sisters. And learn money while you're still in the league. Understand money, because you're getting a lot of it. You've still got to be taxed. You've got to pay half of what you make to taxes. You've got to understand that. If you don't understand something, you're going to lose it.

Obviously, Andre chose to make his exit from football, but he advises every player in any sport to own the fact that his career will end and to make plans.

Think about the end. Don't ever think you won't get hurt or get cut or anything like that. Say to yourself, "I have to keep some money for the rest of my life. What can I do to sustain myself?"

I'm just going to continue what I'm doing: buying property, leasing it out, and investing in different companies. I went to school to learn and to learn the language, to learn about how to run businesses and how to get into business, and how to communicate with people. That's what I went to school for. I didn't go to school just to make more money. I went to school to learn how to *manage* my money and then make more with it. But I'm also going to school just to learn more about this society, this world, because I didn't know much about anything but football. I missed a lot of life playing football, so I'm just trying to catch up.

FROM THE ATHLETE
Chris McCormack, Legendary Triathlete, on Aging and Being Smart

"Be your own CEO to some degree, and take responsibility for your future. Your ass is not going to age like wine. If you're making sports a profession, you're blessed. Right? You're one of the lucky ones. So understand you're one of the lucky ones. It ain't going to last forever. So by understanding you're a lucky one, you realize, 'I need to be clever with what I'm doing.'

"Be your own CEO, so don't outsource your money to all these people, because I hear about all these athletes that get ripped off and make stupid decisions, buying crazy cars and dumb things. Start putting money into things that you know you're going to require, like paying down your mortgage, buying an investment property that brings in rental income for you.

"While you may have to get a job and you may have to do things on the other side of your sport, you've got a head start—or you've at least maintained where you need to be. My father used to say, 'When you're forty, all of your friends that you finished college with have been twenty years into their careers. They're at the peak of their earning capacity. But you're walking out of your peak and into a trough.'

"Young athletes need to remember that even if you're making millions and millions of dollars, when you retire, you're out in the real world where you're at the bottom, and all your peers are now at the top.

"I encourage people to read on what they should do with their money. Be fiscally responsible. Buying assets that depreciate value is stupid. Set a budget. As athletes, we're the same as any other household. Everyone has to have some sort of fiscal responsibility. Everyone knows how much they make. Everyone knows what they should do. Sure, some people have an air, and want to look good and say, 'I'm an athlete, I need to look a certain way." But whenever you're living a certain way to please the people who like you anyway, your fan base, you're being detrimental to yourself."

MONEY IS FREEDOM

Okay, I'm going to end the book right here and just send you to talk to Andre Hal. Seriously. That gentleman has got it all figured out. He's going to be CEO of his own real estate conglomerate one day or maybe president of the United States. But one thing he said to me still rings especially true: "If you don't understand something, you're going to lose it."

That's the essence of what I'm sharing with you. Yes, you need a team; yes, you need to listen to experts. But it's your life. It's your money. It's your future. If you're not educated and aware of what's going on, and if you're not making decisions that work for you, someone else will make decisions about *your* money that work for *them*. My Financial Literacy for Athletes video course at WealthLit101.com is a great place to start. More than twenty short, easy-to-watch videos full of essentials and useful tips will help you be ready to take charge of your finances.

You see, money is freedom. Freedom to end your career on your own terms instead of being cut and going from team to team begging for a job or trying to hang on in tournaments or races after it's obvious your skills have faded. Freedom to have the life you want after you retire, whether that's a high-powered life as an entrepreneur or real estate mogul or a quiet life of speaking, coaching, and spending time with your family. Freedom from worry and anxiety about money and security. All this planning, self-discipline, team-building, and education I've been going on about has only one real purpose:

To position you to enjoy the freedom you want when you want it.

Think of the power you have when you're in a strong financial position. You can choose not to accept a poor contract offer because you don't need the money. You can walk away from a questionable business deal because you're not desperate. You can quit your sport completely if you no longer have the passion to play it. Money equals choices, and when you're retired by thirty-seven with your whole life in front of you, you want choices. And you ensure that you have the choices you want by *planning your exit now*.

HOW TO EXIT WELL

What does it mean to exit well? Well, in one of my other books, I advise business owners who aspire to sell their companies to start planning for a sale from the moment they open the doors. For professional athletes, that means from the time you start your career, you should be thinking about what happens when that career is over:

- How will you make the financial transition to LAS (life after sport)?
- How will you make the psychological transition, which can be even tougher?
- What will you live on?
- Will you take a break or jump right into something new?
- Are you putting together a team to help you?
- Do you have a plan for what comes next?

For business owners, exiting well means primarily two things: maximizing the value of the business so you can sell it for the best price possible and making sure the company's set up so it doesn't miss a beat after you walk out the door.

It's no different for athletes. You want to maximize your value during your career so you can earn as much as possible from salary, endorsements, and the like, and you want to maximize your post-career value by doing things like networking and growing your social media audience. And you want to make sure you're set up so you don't miss a beat: money in the bank, little to no debt, a strong support system, and an array of new ventures and projects to keep you engaged and produce new streams of income.

What does a "good exit" look like? It's different depending on your age, sport, income, and goals, but here are some of the basics:

- You have a substantial amount of money saved and invested that you can live on.
- You have little debt.
- You have no legal or tax judgments hanging over your head.
- You have a solid reputation in your sport and the community.
- You are physically and psychologically healthy.
- You have projects in the works and things to look forward to.

Financial milestones for a good exit include having enough cash saved to cover at least one year's worth of living expenses based on your current budget, having debt service payments equal to no more than 20 percent of your income (so if you gross $30,000 a month, you should be spending no more than $6,000 of that paying off credit card and car loan balances), and having all federal, state, and local taxes current. Personal milestones include having areas of interest that you're passionate about and having time to unwind from the demands of your sport. The goal is to minimize surprises while giving you time to pursue wellness in body and mind and manage the transition from one stage of your life to the next.

Former Duke and NBA star Grant Hill, who hung up the sneakers in 2013, is an example of how to do it right. Always a poised, smart player, Hill not only started building relationships during his career that led to a mezzanine fund (a fund that invests in start-up companies seeking a second round of capital to fuel growth) and real estate holdings but also began building a world-class collection of works by African American artists that's worth millions today. That's financial security, opportunities in place ready to build on, and personal passion. That's how you walk away on your terms.

A BAD EXIT

A bad exit, on the other hand, starts with fear, depression, and even panic. The athlete might be in denial that his career is drawing to a close, and that not only keeps him running around in desperation, trying to hang on, but also keeps him from making plans for the next stage. Athletes who won't or can't contemplate the end of their careers frequently have messy financial lives, including:

- Little or no savings
- Lots of debt
- Few post-play career or business prospects
- A messy personal life—divorce, child support, lots of hangers-on
- A less-than-ideal brand, which makes it harder to land endorsements

I'm not suggesting that all athletes who fail to save money or invest during their careers also have ugly personal lives, only that not thinking about the future can make you reckless. You assume that if things are fine today, they'll always be fine tomorrow, and we know that's not true in the volatile world of pro sports. Athletes who refuse to look at the end or plan for their exits tend to have messy, chaotic personal and financial situations that put them at risk of major post-career setbacks, from IRS audits to bankruptcy to criminal prosecution.

Irrepressible, immensely talented NFL Hall of Fame wide receiver Terrell Owens was a joy to watch on the field. Off the field was more of a problem. Toward what was obviously the end, he tried desperately to get a job with a team to no avail, settling for a final season with the Allen Wranglers of the Indoor Football League in 2012. Several years back he had claimed that his financial advisors had lured him into some unsuccessful investments, but his financial woes probably had something to do with his $44,600 monthly child support payments. Joe Kozlowski at Sportscasting.com estimates that Owens ended up burning through nearly $80 million.

That's why I counsel my athlete clients to think of themselves as businesses. When you're running a business, there's no room for chaos or chasing impossible dreams. You make plans, you have a Plan B in case things go sideways, and you stick to the plan. That's how stars like QB Andrew Luck and Yankee reliever Mariano Rivera get to go out on their terms.

A DEATH IN THE FAMILY

Boxer Sugar Ray Leonard was a joy to watch in the ring, but he had a great deal of trouble letting go when his career seemed to be at an end. He staged multiple comebacks in the 1990s, including victories against "Marvelous" Marvin Hagler and the less marvelous Donny Lalonde. But Leonard never seemed happy. Apart from fighting addiction, he also mourned the loss of boxing from his life, a sadness he shared on NPR:

> Of all the things I miss in boxing, I miss the preparation of a bout, I miss choreographing tactics and moves and things like that. I miss all of my guys, my entourage being around me and working out with me, getting in better shape . . . it's a gradual progression of getting better, and, as weeks go by, you look into the mirror and you see a different person. It evolves. One minute, you look kind of soft, and then, within six to eight weeks, your muscle and all that definition appears. The mirror doesn't lie. It tells you exactly what you are.

For many pro athletes, the psychological toll that retirement takes is devastating, more so even than the financial cost. Overnight, you're out of the tribe. Your reason for getting up in the morning for the last twenty years is gone. The camaraderie of the locker room or clubhouse is replaced by the unbearable quiet of your living room. The adrenaline of competition? That's history. It's a seismic event that many athletes are simply not prepared for, and when you add the fear and panic that can come with not being financially prepared, it's hardly surprising that some studies suggest that retired athletes are more susceptible to depression than the rest of the population.

As his ten-year career as an NFL tight end was coming to a close, Ben Hartsock was concerned about post-career ennui, so he made a quick transition into a career as a sports agent. In an interview with Front Office Sports, he admitted, "Had I not jumped right into working, I wouldn't have been able to handle it. I could have downward spiraled."

Hartsock says the experience of retirement for the pro athlete—at a young age, usually involuntary, often while believing they can still contribute—is uniquely devastating. "I don't know what other industry or business has a similar experience," he said in that same interview. "The shelf life of an athlete is limited in a way I can't think any other profession is. Think about going to high school getting great marks, going to college and excelling, and after five or ten years of being the best surgeon in the world, they take it away from you. That's hard."

It's bad enough when your salary checks stop and companies are no longer interested in signing you to endorsement deals. But what really makes retirement devastating for so many athletes is the loss of identity. Without your sport and your team and your routine, who are you? It really feels like a death in the family.

Brett Flanigan comments:

Remember Lindsey Vonn, the skier? She had a documentary made about her, and I've heard her speak, and it made me feel really sad about the level of depression that she went into [when she had to retire]. Now, put that in perspective. Lindsey Vonn is someone we remember, but the guy who's on the offensive line, it's exactly the same for him when he's done. There are issues that the second- and third- and fourth- and fiftieth-tier players suffer from, and no one will ever know that they're suffering. But they do, and some of them have money. But they're just shattered people.

Brett explains the addictive high of sports this way: "Imagine you're playing football at Louisiana State University. There are probably a hundred thousand people at the game, millions watching it on TV, every week. For some of those guys playing for LSU, they've had that for four years. And then, if they're not good enough to make the NFL, then that's the end for them. They can bounce around the Canadian league if they want, but there's no money in that. Those guys will basically never play football again. How do you do that?"

MAKE YOUR PITCH

In other words, how do you keep going when the lights go off, the big checks stop rolling in, and nobody wants your autograph anymore? My approach is called PITCH, an appropriately sports-themed acronym that covers the five elements professional athletes should be clear on or have firmly in place at least twelve months before they leave their sport:

- **P = Purpose.** What's going to give meaning to your life after sports? What will get you out of bed in the morning? Financial concerns can overwhelm the question of meaning, but more than most people, pro athletes need a reason to keep going. After all, you've spent decades with one focus: doing whatever you had to do to win. Now, that's over. As you near the end of your career, start thinking about what lights you up. What do you enjoy? What are you passionate about? What would you do if no one ever paid you a dime? Is there a cause that you care about deeply, whether it's climate change or Black Lives Matter? Once you've found some of those answers, start exploring ways you could work your passions into your postretirement life.

- **I = Income.** This is basic. Unless you have deferred salary coming to you, your team salary or event winnings are going to be *over*. Gone. How will you live? If you haven't been thinking about that, time to start. The key questions to ask are pretty basic:

- » How much will you need to earn per month in retirement to enjoy your lifestyle?
- » What sources of income do you have now that will continue in retirement, like endorsements and appearance fees?
- » What new sources of income do you need to fill that gap? These might include getting a job, broadcasting, speaking, coaching, income from rental properties, stock dividends, and royalties from licensing your name or likeness.
- » What do you need to do to begin pursuing those other sources of income?

My advice: pursue every possible source of income you're interested in because not all of them will pan out. Start while you're still active because some opportunities take time, and you don't want to reach the end of your playing career, which is tough enough, only to confront a 50 percent cut in pay overnight.

- **T = Tribe.** One of the loneliest, most isolating aspects of retirement for many pro athletes, especially the ones who play team sports, is losing the camaraderie of the team. These are men or women whom you're with for six, seven, eight, maybe even nine months out of the year. You train together, sweat together, eat together, win together, and lose together. You're more than a team; you're a band of brothers (or sisters). You know the feeling. Once you retire, you lose that tribe, and that can be devastating. So before you hang 'em up for the last time, figure out who your new tribe will be. Will it be a team of people starting a new company? That's perfect. Start-ups often come with the same balls-to-the-wall sense of camaraderie as sports. What about an entrepreneurship networking group, your church, or even a support group for retired athletes? Give some serious thought to who will be in your tribe, and if there isn't a retired pro support group in your area, maybe think about starting one.

- **C = Challenge.** Most athletes are adrenaline junkies. You spend years getting in premium condition and then going out and defying the odds. Then you retire and everything is mundane. Let's face it, there's not a lot of "thrill of victory" in taking the kids to school, mowing the lawn, and grilling steaks. So while you might want to enjoy the quiet life after years of work, it's also important to channel your athlete's drive and competitiveness by finding a new challenge for yourself. Start a business. Learn a skill. Get your master's degree. Build a home addition yourself. Train for a marathon. Have a plan for the challenges you'll tackle once you're out of your sport and have free time.

- **H = Home.** Be it ever so humble, et cetera. A healthy, loving, welcoming home life is the center of everything. Home means the people who lift you up when you're feeling lost and down because you miss your teammates. It's the place in which you plan out your next ventures, celebrate big milestones, and chill with some close friends on a summer night. Home is everything, so as you move toward retirement, make sure it's strong. Is your relationship with your significant other strained after years of being on the road? Maybe it's time for some counseling. Do you have long-term houseguests who've worn out their welcome? Evict them. Is your home large and comfortable enough for your growing family? Plan your move while you're playing and have a healthy income. Home should be a haven, a resort—Robert Frost wrote, "Home is the place that when you have to go there, they have to take you in." Make sure you have that place.

KNOW THE SCORE

When you retire, it might feel like you're alone, but you're not. There are many resources built to help retired athletes find new direction and thrive after their careers are over. Here are a few:

- Athletes for Care (athletesforcare.org)

- Athlete Career Transition (athletecareertransition.com)
- Crossing the Line (crossingthelinesport.com)
- Athletes Soul (athletessoul.space)
- The Final Whistle
- Athlete Transition Services (atscorp.org)
- Arizona State Global Sport Institute (globalsport.asu.edu/resources/athlete-transitions)
- Athletes Connected (athletesconnected.umich.edu)

THE HANDOFF

It should be clear by now that for any professional athlete, the goal is a clean, smooth transition from a life centered on sports to a more balanced life—one where the income and all-consuming culture of sports is replaced with multiple sources of income, planning for the future, and a new, healthy sense of purpose and community. I call that the Handoff. My goal is to help you make the Handoff with minimal disruption.

There are many keys to a successful Handoff, but everything hinges on your AES. Earlier in the book I told you about the AES, the organizational structure for your one-person business with your CMO, COO, and CFO at the center. This is where it all comes together. The point of the AES and your team is to organize every facet of your life and finances according to the guidelines we've talked about so that when you get to the end of your career, to your Handoff, it's a welcome beginning to a new stage of your life, not a dreaded fall into obscurity and isolation.

My goal is that by the time you reach your own Handoff, you'll be looking forward to the future, not worried about money, and have things to be excited about, like meetings with business partners, projects, or commercial shoots. You'll finally have time to spend with friends and take a vacation. It will be a time of possibility, not mourning.

A few essentials have to be in place before that can happen. Your Board of Directors should have been in place for years by the time you retire, so they work together as smoothly as a veteran second baseman and shortstop turning a double play. You should have grown your wealth by saving and investing according to the plan I've given you. You have a nice nest egg of emergency cash tucked away, along with a diversified portfolio of investments being carefully managed by your CFO. You have the insurance you need, a comprehensive estate and charitable giving plan, and little or no debt. You might even have your five-year brand development plan laid out along with the financial opportunities you plan to pursue: "buy and flip" properties, franchises, licensed products, some venture investing, and so on.

THE AES IN ACTION

If you have all these essentials in order, then you're in good shape to implement the AES. With the chart below, you can see how the AES works to address each component of your sports, financial, and business life as you move closer to retirement and start your next act. The AES is designed to take you through each of the four phases of the Handoff:

1. Preretirement, three or more years out from the end of your current contract or the date you've decided to retire

2. Countdown, one year out from retirement

3. Handoff, the three months immediately after you retire

4. Retirement, the rest of your life

For the purposes of using the AES, assume that your current team contract will be your last one (always a wise thing to assume), even if it's your first. If you're an individual athlete who doesn't do team contracts, use three years of earnings as a benchmark for the AES. If your career lasts more than three additional years, that's great, but if at the end of three years you have all your plans in place, then whenever retirement comes, you'll be ready.

Without further ado, here's the AES fully fleshed out.

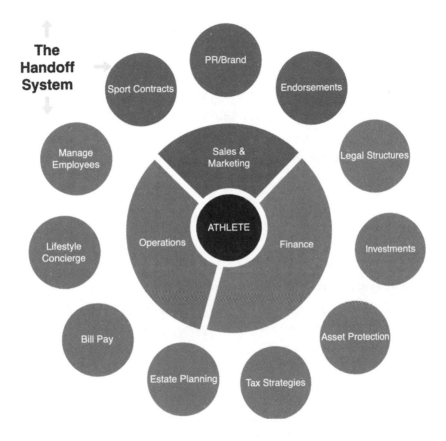

That's you in the center, the CEO. You, the athlete, drive all this financial and business activity. In the second ring are the three major players in your AES: your CMO, CFO, and COO. In the outermost ring, we have the concerns that each department manages:

- **Legal structures** is the LLCs, corporations, and other entities set up on your behalf.

- **Investments** represents everything from stocks to hedge funds to retirement accounts to buying equity in a friend's start-up. It also includes liquid assets like cash and CDs.

- **Asset protection** is about making sure your assets aren't unjustly taken by creditors. This could be accomplished by insurance, trusts, legal structures, and so on.

- **Tax strategies** references comprehensive tax planning designed to minimize your tax burden while ensuring that all taxes are paid on time.

- **Estate planning** encompasses not only your will and any trusts but your charitable giving plan as well.

- **Bill pay** refers to the automatic payment of all your bills by your CPA or business manager.

- **Lifestyle concierge** is a fancy name for the person—your valet, your business manager, perhaps a personal assistant—who manages the details of your daily life, from making appointments to making travel plans to confirming meetings and making sure everyone signs your NDA.

- **Manage employees** is about dealing with the pay, benefits, tax filings, legal matters, termination and hiring of any personnel in your employ—your Board of Directors, housekeepers, chef, trainer, personal assistant, and the like.

- **Sport contracts** refers to your agent's work in negotiating your contracts as well as ensuring that the terms of the contracts are met while advising you on dos and don'ts.

- **PR/branding** covers all activities that impact your brand and public image: press coverage, social media activity, charitable work, commercials, endorsements, and so on. Your agent may collaborate with your publicist here.

- **Endorsements** encompasses the contracts, negotiations, payment, and activities related to your endorsement deals, including personal appearances and the conditions of your contracts.

Simple, right? Well, no. However, you'll have help, and paying attention to these eleven areas of need before, during, and after your Handoff will give you the best chance of having everything you need in place to enjoy a prosperous late career, a smooth transition to civilian life, and a fantastic "after-career."

The idea behind the AES is that as you move into each stage of the Handoff, you fill in the details for each of the eleven areas of importance—choosing investments, hiring key people, and so on. That way, you're attending to every piece of your financial and business life in real time, so nothing's overlooked as you head toward retirement. Accounts are fully funded, investments made, taxes filed, and endorsements put in place.

For each phase of the Handoff, you'll want to walk through each area in the system with your team and run a systems check. What does your investment portfolio look like, and does it need to be rebalanced? Are you taking full advantage of all the tax breaks you get from running a charity? Do you need to hire someone? Fire someone? Pay payroll tax? Is one of your endorsement contracts nearing its end, meaning you need to seek a new sponsor? Do you need to replenish your liquid savings because you recently had a large emergency cash outlay? Do you have an important television interview to prepare for?

The AES isn't a static document. It's a checklist that reminds you to attend to these critical areas of your financial and business life and to check in on them and update them at least once per quarter. Most of these concerns won't change very much over time—for instance, you'll always want to make sure you have sufficient insurance—but some will adjust as you draw closer to the Handoff and then pass into retirement. So let's look at those.

FROM THE ATHLETE

Solomon Wilcots, Former NFL Player and Broadcaster, on Career Transitions

"My mentor, who had become my attorney, had seen me do television work locally while I was a player. He knew I wanted to do it. So when I was done playing and I was working in insurance, I remember him coming to my cubicle—I didn't have an office—and saying, 'You should be working in television.'

"I said, 'I've put all these years in here; this is what I thought I would be working in, and now you're telling me I shouldn't do it?' He says, 'You can always come back and work here. But if you don't give this a try, you'll be kicking yourself the rest of your life.' He threw down the gauntlet, challenged me because he knew where my heart was, and boy was he right.

"I went and I looked at all the television stations, and none of them would hire me. The local NBC affiliate said, 'Okay, we'll bring you in as an unpaid intern. And I walked away from my other job. I had just retired as a player. I was logging tape, and then I became a writer, and then a producer, and then a reporter. Then I got to be the local weekend anchor. But I worked for two years for free."

Preretirement—Three Years Out

You're still earning pro athlete money, so the focus here is on saving, paying off debts, and exploring investment opportunities. Your main goal is to have multiple new streams of nonsport income in place before you retire, and that begins here. If you have any shot at locking up endorsement deals that will carry over beyond your playing career, this is also the time to explore those.

Countdown—One Year Out

Assuming you've been doing things right for the last two years, this is the time to clean house. Make sure bills are paid, taxes are filed, debts are minimal, and deals are signed. If you're looking at starting a company or investing in someone else's start-up—something where you might have daily involvement—this is the time to get those wheels turning. Also, have your agent review your contract to check on things like your eligibility for league retirement programs or pensions. This would also be a good time to let go any employees who aren't working out so you have time to hire and train replacements. Finally, your income may be dropping soon, so if you can cut costs, do it. Downsizing might not be an option, but things like eating out less and shopping at Costco might be.

Handoff—Three Months Before and After Retirement

You've already done the financial, legal, personnel, and contractual heavy lifting, so this is a time to focus on yourself. No matter how prepared you think you are for retirement, it's still going to be a shock. Set aside funds for a family vacation. Ensure that you have a strong personal assistant on the job so you can take some time for yourself. But—make sure you have meetings on the docket for your new company or real estate venture. If there are shows, interviews, or ESPN training you'd like to do, have your publicist set those up. Go through the must-do items for this early period in your retirement so you don't forget anything.

Retirement

Now you're in maintenance mode. You've established the baseline for your savings, investments, business ventures, and all the rest, so from here on out, it's about meeting with your team and making adjustments as conditions change and your goals change. How are your business ventures doing? Is it time to cut bait on some and look into something new? Do you have a passion that you want to pursue? Is there a charitable cause newly on your radar around which you'd like to explore a new foundation? What's your tribe up to? How are you evolving your brand? What are your goals for five, ten, and twenty years after retirement?

One phase of the Handoff leads into the next, but if matters are taken care of with expertise and attention to detail, each phase is also easier. Some sections could become irrelevant as time passes; for instance, when you retire, you could replace "Sports Contracts" with "Speaking & Appearances" since you'll have more time for both.

Working together with your Board of Directors, spouse, banker, insurance broker, tax expert, and a few others, you'll be able to map out every stage of your life and career for the next twenty years if you choose. That will put you in position to build wealth, preserve wealth, protect your loved ones, and build a future you can really enjoy.

THE HANDOFF SURVEY

But completing the AES and being ready for your Handoff takes work and preparation. Have you done the work? Are you ready? You could guess, or you could take the Handoff Survey, reproduced here but found at WealthLit101.com. The survey assesses where you are in your preparation for a prosperous financial and business future. Answer the 30 questions on a 1–5 scale, and calculate your total Win Score. The key below tells you what that score means and what your next steps should be.

WEALTHLIT.COM "HANDOFF" SURVEY

Age

Marital status

Estimated years until retirement from sport

Average 5-year salary

Current endorsement income

Please answer the following questions on a 1–5 scale—1 for strongly disagree, 5 for strongly agree.

1. I have consistently saved at least 25 percent of my income for the future.

   1 ☐ 2 ☐ 3 ☐ 4 ☐ 5 ☐

2. My debt is under control.

   1 ☐ 2 ☐ 3 ☐ 4 ☐ 5 ☐

3. My taxes are up to date and prepared by a professional experienced with athlete taxation.

   1 ☐ 2 ☐ 3 ☐ 4 ☐ 5 ☐

4. My monthly expenses are under control.

   1 ☐ 2 ☐ 3 ☐ 4 ☐ 5 ☐

5. I have sufficient insurance coverage (life, disability, umbrella).

   1 ☐ 2 ☐ 3 ☐ 4 ☐ 5 ☐

6. I have an estate plan.

1 □ 2 □ 3 □ 4 □ 5 □

7. I have clear financial goals for the next 5 years.

1 □ 2 □ 3 □ 4 □ 5 □

8. I have clear financial goals for the next 10 years.

1 □ 2 □ 3 □ 4 □ 5 □

9. I have clear goals for what I want my life to look like when I retire.

1 □ 2 □ 3 □ 4 □ 5 □

10. I am actively pursuing business opportunities with partners.

1 □ 2 □ 3 □ 4 □ 5 □

11. I am relying on professionals, not friends or family, to handle my finances.

1 □ 2 □ 3 □ 4 □ 5 □

12. I say no to family members and friends who ask for financial assistance.

1 □ 2 □ 3 □ 4 □ 5 □

13. I have clear goals for what I want my life to look like when I retire.

1 □ 2 □ 3 □ 4 □ 5 □

14. I have charitable projects I would like to pursue.

1 □ 2 □ 3 □ 4 □ 5 □

15. I have assembled my financial Board of Directors.

1 □ 2 □ 3 □ 4 □ 5 □

16. I have avoided financial troubles like bankruptcies, loan defaults, and tax liens.

1 □ 2 □ 3 □ 4 □ 5 □

17. I have excellent credit.

1 □ 2 □ 3 □ 4 □ 5 □

18. I am pursuing or plan to pursue additional education in finance and business.

1 □ 2 □ 3 □ 4 □ 5 □

19. I have a decent, "Finance 101" understanding of the stock market, investing, and debt.

1 □ 2 □ 3 □ 4 □ 5 □

20. I am disciplined financially.

1 □ 2 □ 3 □ 4 □ 5 □

21. I have a solid reputation and the ability to tell my friends "No" about lending money.

1 □ 2 □ 3 □ 4 □ 5 □

22. I am willing to listen to advice from financial, tax, business, and legal professionals, even when I don't agree with it.

1 □ 2 □ 3 □ 4 □ 5 □ .

23. I welcome regular communication from my Board of Directors and other advisors.

1 □ 2 □ 3 □ 4 □ 5 □

24. I want a comprehensive plan for my financial and business future.

1 □ 2 □ 3 □ 4 □ 5 □

25. I am willing to take risks.

1 □ 2 □ 3 □ 4 □ 5 □

26. I am willing to trust people.

1 □ 2 □ 3 □ 4 □ 5 □

27. I do not base my lifestyle or purchasing decisions on what my peers are doing.

1 □ 2 □ 3 □ 4 □ 5 □

28. I have something in mind that will bring me purpose and meaning after I retire.

1 ☐ 2 ☐ 3 ☐ 4 ☐ 5 ☐

29. My reputation in the community and among my fans is excellent.

1 ☐ 2 ☐ 3 ☐ 4 ☐ 5 ☐

30. I have a strong professional and business network outside of my sport.

1 ☐ 2 ☐ 3 ☐ 4 ☐ 5 ☐

SCORING: 30–150

121–150	Champion	You're already in great shape for your future.
91–120	Contender	You're solid but could probably use some guidance.
61–90	Bench Warmer	You've got a lot of work to do. Get busy.
30–60	Cellar Dweller	If you get hurt tomorrow, you're in a lot of trouble.

The survey isn't meant to unnerve you but rather to let you know where you are in terms of being prepared to turn the volatile, unpredictable life of a pro athlete into a bright future. If you were honest and scored low, that just means you need to take action. Start now. Talk to teammates or peers about who manages their finances and get a referral. Start reading and learning. Ask successful retired athletes for their secrets. There's a lot to do, but there's a great deal of opportunity out there for pro athletes that's not open to anyone else.

You're unique. You really are blessed . . . with opportunity. Use it. Get started now, and if you need more resources, go to WealthLit101.com to check out my Financial Literacy for Athletes video course.

Now, go be a winner.